SHOOTING THE RAT

SHOOTING THE RAT

Stories and Poems by Outstanding High School Writers

Edited by
Mark Pawlak and Dick Lourie
With Ron Schreiber and Robert Hershon

Hanging Loose Press
Brooklyn, New York

Published by Hanging Loose Press, 231 Wyckoff Street, Brooklyn, NY 11217-2208. All rights reserved. No part of this book may be reproduced without the publisher's written permission, except for brief quotations in reviews.

www.hangingloosepress.com

Printed in the United States of America
10 9 8 7 6 5 4 3 2 1

Hanging Loose Press thanks the Literature Program of the New York State Council on the Arts for a grant in support of the publication of this book.

Cover painting by Jesse Cohen
Cover design by Pamela Flint

Acknowledgments: The editors wish to thank the many teachers and poets who stay on the watch for excellent high school writers and point them our way. Happily, there are more than we can name here. We would like to extend special thanks to Nikki Paley, who did a great deal of the early and arduous organizational work on this anthology, and Charles Luce, Chair of the Art Department at Saint Ann's School, who introduced us to Jesse Cohen's extraordinary cover painting.

Library of Congress Cataloging-in-Publication Data

Shooting the rat: stories and poems by outstanding high school
   writers / edited by Mark Pawlak and Dick Lourie.
    p. cm.
   ISBN 1-931236-24-0 --ISBN 1-931236-23-2 (pbk.)
   1. High School students' writings, American. 2. High school
students--Literary collections. 3. Teenagers' writings, American.
4. School prose, American. 5. School verse, American. I. Pawlak,
Mark. II. Lourie, Dick.

PS508.S43S54 2003
810.8'09283--dc21

                                                          2003040748

Produced at The Print Center, Inc., 225 Varick St., New York, NY 10014, a non-profit facility for literary and arts-related publications. (212) 206-8465

Contents

IV In My Grandmother's House

V Welcome

VI Figure It Out

Introduction

What do you get when you combine a precociously mature artistic sensibility with the realities of life as an adolescent in America? *Hanging Loose* magazine has been providing answers to that question by publishing the work of high school age writers for more than 35 years.

In 1966, when we started our literary magazine, we decided to publish poems and stories by gifted high school poets and fiction writers alongside that of adults, in every issue. To our knowledge, we are the only literary magazine in the United States to have made that commitment, which we have maintained ever since. And we hold these young aspirants to the same high standards as our adult contributors; the result is that we have established a reputation for publishing high school work of remarkable quality. Wide public recognition of this quality came several years ago when a Hanging Loose poem by a high school writer Jendi Reiter was selected for inclusion in *The Best American Poetry*. This annual anthology celebrating excellence in poetry is not an anthology of high school work, but a selection from the best American poets writing today. And this distinction proved to be more than a one-time exception. The next time, for the 1996 edition of *The Best American Poetry*, editor and distinguished poet Adrienne Rich chose four of our high school poems: Natasha Le Bel's "Boxing the Female" and "Foot Fire Burn Dance," Quentin Rowan's "Prometheus in Coney Island," and Deborah Stein's "Heat." Readers of *Shooting the Rat* can judge for themselves, since we have, of course, proudly included all of them here.

In 1988, we ourselves began sharing the work of our young writers more widely, by initiating a series of anthologies drawn from the high school section of *Hanging Loose* magazine. The first two volumes in the series, *Smart Like Me* and *Bullseye*, present poetry and fiction that appeared in our high school section between 1966 and 1994. This third volume brings us to the present.

Whenever we publish one of these anthologies, we take advantage of the opportunity to get back in touch with our authors and see what they've been up to since graduating from high school. We're always pleased to find how many have stuck with writing. In putting together *Shooting the Rat* we found, for example, that many went on to win awards in college for writing poetry, fiction, plays; that some have continued to publish in such places as *The Paris Review*, *The Kenyon Review*, *The Black Warrior Review*; and that one, Alison Stine, has had a chapbook collection of poems published by a university press (see the contributors' notes for full details).

And, over the years since *Smart Like Me*, several of our young authors have gone on to become professional writers. There are also some who have stayed in touch all along, continuing to show us their work as it matured, and "matriculating" out of our high school section into the regular pages of the magazine. In fact, seven poets who first appeared in our high school section have gone on to publish collections of their own from Hanging Loose Press.

The poems and stories presented in this anthology are among the most recent work from the long Hanging Loose tradition of fine high school writing, published in our magazine between 1994 and 2002. We are proud to bring them to you.

* * *

Contributors of the 170 selections in *Shooting the Rat* represent 21 states (ranging from Vermont to New York to Minnesota to Kansas to Texas to California) and Scotland. Their backgrounds are varied and disparate. Besides the obvious—they were all teenagers when they wrote these pieces—what do they have in common? Put another way, what makes this a unified collection rather than 170 single pieces? As editors putting this anthology together, we wrestled with these questions.

The answers, we discovered, lie in the shared experience of becoming and being an adolescent in our society. We therefore shaped the book to reflect that idea; each of its six sections brings together some aspect of that shared experience.

The book opens with Gemma Cooper-Novack's poem, "Shooting the Rat," which gives the collection its title. This is a brilliant, witty, and somewhat mischievous meditation on following directions, which, she tells us, is frequently not as easy as it may seem. Adolescents, of course, are accustomed to getting instructions from parents, teachers, and adults at large—and surely part of being an adolescent is the growing realization that there's more than one way to understand, interpret, and carry out what you're being told to do, or think. Who's telling you, and why? Will these instructions, in the end, benefit you? Does obedience to instruction always yield the predictable results envisioned by the instructor? And, in a way, her opening line might ironically sum up, from the adolescent's point of view, something about the way those giving the instructions seem to see the whole enterprise of being a teenager: "It was a simple action...."

Each section of the book likewise takes its title from the poem that opens it. The first, "Pears of the World," brings together poems in which the writer is an observer—but not simply an objective bystander. Like Sarah Nooter's pears, the world invites these young poets to dig in and participate in the sensory riches it has to offer.

There is, says William Lopez, "a wing in my mouth." In this second section, we see poems equally interested in the world, but here more consciously reflecting on the poet's own presence, and on the awakening young poet's realization that, using the tools of their own art, artists can wield the power to shape what they themselves experience.

The third section, "Tell Them It's a Potato," is about the writer's encounters with another world, the one that exists not "out there," but somewhere inside, the world of art, and of books. Julie Scharper's opening poem takes on the creative writing class: how to make "use a metaphor" more than a rote instruction about literary technique. These adolescent poets are responding for the first time to the world of adult literature and history, to Shakespeare, Picasso, Virgil—Their responses are not book reports, but works of art in themselves.

Section four, "In My Grandmother's House," brings together poems and stories about family. Family is observed, celebrated, teased, criticized, bemoaned, humored, mourned—predictably, the emotional range is broad. Parents are here, brothers and sisters; and a surprising number of grandparents—teenagers, some have observed, often feel close to their parents' parents. The section opens and closes with moving tributes, very different from each other, to grandmothers, by Ben Lerner and Alexis Goldberg.

The theme of the next section, "Welcome," is the nature of the adolescent's precarious transition from being a child to being an adult. As an opening for this section, we couldn't resist Susan Currie's poem, with its astonishing opening line: "She watched the circus burn that day."

Shooting the Rat closes with a section which is—perhaps not surprisingly—the longest. "Figure It Out" deals with awakening sexuality: What's happening now? What's ahead of me as an adult? And: What am I leaving behind? As an opening selection, Drew Tarlow's joyful little poem might sum up what the pieces here are about: "exploring."

***

At Hanging Loose we are always excited about the high school writers whose work we publish. As this collection was going to press, issue number 82 of *Hanging Loose* magazine was in production. As with every issue since 1966, it includes some extraordinary pieces by high school age writers. We're pleased that in this respect our magazine hasn't changed in all these years.

But some things about high school writing in general have changed since we began. Happily, it's no longer true that—as Richard Lewis noted in his introduction to *Smart Like Me*, the first volume in this series—*Hanging Loose* represents one of the very few opportunities for high school writers to share their work widely. There are, for example, a number of summer workshops for high schoolers; and the Poets and Writers organization in New York City issues an annual directory of resources for aspiring high school writers.

Another change since our inception in 1966 is that increasing numbers of poets and English teachers have viewed their students as potential writers, and nurtured them toward that end. Arts councils in many states, and independent organizations like Teachers & Writers Collaborative in New York City, have provided resources and materials to assist these efforts.

And *Hanging Loose* has benefited as well from this extension of interest in high school writing. We rely on the expertise of poets and teachers around the country who must be doing something very right in their teaching and nurturing: Their students consistently turn out much more than their share of the wonderful high school writing that appears in our pages. They know who they are—and we are grateful for their work in developing young writers.

As for us at HL, we intend to keep at it just as long as the terrific poems and stories keep coming our way. Readers of *Shooting the Rat* who are of high school age are encouraged to send us their work directly to consider for publication. Special guidelines for high school writers are also posted on our website at hangingloosepress.com. Help us keep the tradition alive.

Gemma Cooper-Novack

Shooting the Rat

"Describe and evoke a simple action (for example, sharpening a pencil, carving a tombstone, shooting a rat)."
—John Gardner, writing exercises

It was a simple action:
one twitch of a finger and blood and fur
sprayed over the room. To our white walls and carpet,
the Jackson Pollock gun added dirty brown
for a textured masterwork; bits of whisker
were wedged in the door's ivory hinges. We cleaned all afternoon
and kept on going, into the night
and on through the morning, vacuuming pencil shavings
from the carpet, cutting our feet
on bits of stone (enough blood
in this room already.) We scrubbed at the walls
with soap and cold water, rubbed circular motions
on the floor with Resolve. With a toothpick
we pushed the pink nose from our keyhole, used plaster
to close off the crack in the baseboard. It was a simple
action, and we fell back on the white couch, exhausted,
out of bullets when the mice came in through the ceiling.

I
Pears of the World

Sarah Nooter

Pears of the World

We, the pears of the world,
would like for you to eat us
whole. We want you to peel us,
to boil us, to poach us. Smother
us in the milk of raspberries. Singe
us with molten chocolate.

Grow us, pick us,
wash and slice us,
chew us,
tell us when we're too ripe
and too dry.
No, really.

Phoebe Prioleau

On the Corner of Fulton and Liberty

The woman in the
Contact-lens blue
Suit and matching stilettos catches her
Heel in the
Subway grating
At rush hour. She
Crouches, half
Barefoot, tugs
Three times as legs
Pass her by.
The shoe pops out—
Lucky! She
Didn't want
Anything more.

Elizabeth Bear

Driving Home at Night After Picking Up the Milk

A heron flew over the road and the car
by the neighbor's pond.
The headlights caught her white underbelly
brush of wide wings a small moon rising.
She must've been there fishing
long neck dipping to snip at the flicking tails
stilt legs treading through muddy water.
The drought left a wet smell at the bank,
grass reached towards the cracked mud.
The sun set with the rising wind that pushed rain
into Texas for the first time in five months.
She never did find a fish slow enough
for her to swallow.
She could pull herself away easily
raising those great feathers to the sky
skimming the water's surface as though she was the air
herself a bit of down instead of a great body.
She was a ghost too on the road home
another incomplete thought
one more unknown in the rearview mirror.

Katina Antoniades

1920

in a blue and white dress

she streams by on the sidewalk

the rain
and the night as soft as a dog's ear

Katina Antoniades

Poem at a Quarter to Six

my mind
winds rope
around the
stars & planets
to keep them together

Katrina Antoniades

Windsock

you are a windsock in a trailer park,
the only name I know on an unfamiliar map,
the last number counted between thunder and lightning.

Lauren Brozovich

A 1950s Televised A-Bomb Drill Aired for Educational Purposes

written in response to scenes from the documentary The Atomic Café

In the camera's field of view
schoolchildren collapse
from their seats to the rectangles beneath
their desks, hands folded sepal

fashion over their necks. On the board
there may have been perfect cur-
sive words: sepal, petal, stamen, carpel
and opulent, Georgia O'Keefe chalk diagrams

of flower-ovaled ovaries, at-attention
stamens, the cocktail-straw-thin
pollen tube. On the teacher's desk
there might have even been a blue open-
ed flower with visible insides made

by a send-in science company out of
cloud-painted plastic and pin-stuck foam, pried
apart, hinged, so that the children could look
inside and feel. They may have even been learning

about touch-sensitive plant dynamics,
the spontaneous collapsing of leaves, petals, the whole
propaganda of evolution. *Duck & cover*: fifty
children sliding out of wooden seats into

fifty fetal-positioned 10-year-olds
separated from their at-
home mothers who flash across the screen
diving against kitchen cabinets, cooking
ranges, refrigerator grilles and folding

their dishwater hands prayer-like
over their kerchief-
ed heads, perhaps breathing to God, mouths
pressed against braided rugs, that the
Bleeding Hearts they had felt blossom inside

themselves were as safe in their desk huddles
as this fall-out documentary promised and not as
vulnerable as they looked: retracted
blossom backs huddled over
heavy Easter hearts on a wooden floor
in which no seed could grow.

Lauren Brozovich

In the Girls' Dressing Room Before the Gulling of Beatrice Scene in Shakespeare's *Much Ado About Nothing*

*...Does anyone have a
hair band?* bobby
pins littering
the concrete, balanced half in
pursed mouths
like thermometers, slid into wavy
hair, pinned over the tips of
face-framing braids,
jumbles of white
wire hangers flagged with cleaners'
tickets, Victoria's
Secret bras, and 18th century petticoats,
thin backs wriggling into whale-
bone bustiers, *Can someone help me
get out?* arms signalling
drowning from the tops of over-the-head
dresses, slim waists scratchscrim-
med in voile-&-stays, the
liquid rustle of girl-legs
stepping in and out of acetate
petticoats that stand
free form
like durable meringue lamp
shades, squares of blusher,
blue eye
shadow, thickened
mascara, Neapolitan pink &
blue stage-paint
scuffed over the vague white seats
of full skirts, pantalettes, petticoats...
Can someone curl my hair?
half-done heads sharing
caddies of hot
rollers, stained white gloves, lace
veils, nosegays, a circlet of fake
flowers, camisoles of laundered

paper, Tuscany-smooth
ankles caught up in
Maypole ribbon, flurries of cheek
pinching, blush
brushes, eyelash curlers...
the fabulous-
ness of getting dressed to arrive
breathlessly undressed
onstage in camisoles & tiers of wedding
cake petticoats to fold back over our knees
like bedcovers and ballerina
feet to unbind & slip naked into silver
bowls of freezing water....

Keystone

Fida Fida Fida Fida

They say that firemen are good chefs.
I often see them in the supermarket,
patrolling the produce,
browsing through the spice section.
Their raincoats and helmets
are a strange sight,
standing out like the one little girl on
the carousel who's twice the size of anyone else.
I always knew they would be there before I went inside—
their truck wasn't usually parked on the street.
The firemen sit in their station,
relaxing on couches,
watching *Oprah*
and *Yan Can Cook*
and scribbling down recipes.
One time a firehouse caught fire when the firemen
went out one day to fight another fire.
Some rookie must have burned the muffins.

Matthew Moses

Farmacy

Down on the farmacy
    the personal care items
    lie slightly ajar.
    Moisturizer and Shampoo
    peeking out into their new world
    already instinctively looking
    for some poor soul
    with dry skin and dirty hair.
Down on the farmacy
    the feminine products
    are harvested
    along with transparent deodorants
    and fluorescent toothbrushes.
They say
    pharmers are a rough breed
    waking up before dawn
    to water the condoms
    and milk the shaving cream.
Yesterday Congress passed the
    farmacy bill,
    insuring a brighter-toothed
    shinier-haired, better-smelling America.
They say
    the farmacies are the backbone of
    this beautiful nation.

Julia Kate Jarcho

Iconography

At night the supermarket
is nearly empty. One girl
head heavy
leans on her friends

quietly
with a laugh sometimes.
I have never seen a bird
so perfect in its flight
as she in her unsteady fall.

A wind of lavender hair
covers her eyes. Hunched

she sways in absolute time
with our generation, our ragged
apocalypse, but we can only call her

Sophie, or Violet.

Rebecca Givens

The Twist of Her Head

the twist of her head
was like the dictates of fate
the green of her dress
could cure colds
the sweat
on her brow was the water of Bath
which could bring you health again
you told me this
after a long day of work
your car had broken down
and you were forced to leave it
by the side of the road
find another mode of transportation
search the want ads
for another home
you told me this
as you were crying
how did I get to be such an old man
able to believe that a face
could save me
I saw it only once
on the outbound train

Jenny Jones

Image Retention

She had turned her head away, but I could still see the distant look across her face. It did not dispel her need to talk about it.

All the time that had passed since she'd realised that she had lost him, only now was she able to pin it down to an exact moment. Maybe even a date if she looked back through calendars, diaries of that summer. She put down the coffee mug I had filled for her and began the story, never once looking me in the eye. I knew why. Had she caught my eye, had she caught anyone's eye, the reality of the truth and understanding that lies in the pupil and the iris might have outweighed his importance and sunk her story back to earth. There she would find it so easy and so comfortable to slip again in to dismissing it as imagination, an illusion of her heart. But she continued, driven by the power of her conviction.

It had been a lighthearted summer evening. She was heading out for dinner, going through the motions of forgetting about him. What had passed between them before he left was complicated, she realised that now. But it had been different then. She recalled to me the colour of the sky, watching the rain clouds outside my kitchen window. A deep, golden blue, were her words. She said that she had always known when their paths were about to collide, she could feel it inside her bones. But on this fair summer evening her mind's laughter had silenced her nagging fears of his ghost. But, she half-laughed, feeling his presence in her vicinity did not mean that her stomach maintained its functions on her friend's declaration that he was looming on the horizon. In front of the tartan shop, with a man and a woman she understood were his brother and his brother's girl-friend, without being told.

He looked desperate; he was causing a fuss, waving his arms, emphatically stressing his problem. She did not hear any of the words he was using to explain his difficulty in shopping for wedding presents. His mouth was as blank as a goldfish's to her. His arm actions carried the motion to the flops of blond on his head. As they approached she only halfheartedly answered his polite greetings and enquiries into her well-being. She told me that she had not looked at him once, and that was why she remembered the sky so well...she had looked up at the buildings somewhere to the right of his left shoulder. Image retention. The grey tenement of the upper floors of department stores is still fixed on her retina.

But his eyes were fixed on her. He wasn't taking an interest in her face, or staring at her chest, or looking her up and down...his eyes were all over her body at once. I saw her squirm unconsciously as she described it. She said he was talking to everybody, and sometimes everybody but her, but still his focus did not shift. She had felt the others glance uncomfortably at them as he spoke and she glanced into the distance. She had burned inside and in a moment her body had understood the unfamiliar stare of his intentions, but it had taken until today for her mind to catch up. She sat across the table from me, and I watched realisation making her face look older, sadder and lost in this mystery she had labelled love.

She now realises that in those moments he had understood her. All the months beforehand that she had spent drowning in unrequited love were answered in his five-minute stare. But that stare and those minutes had taken two years to sink past her confusion and self-doubt, to her heart.

In the natural state of panic that her senses had stimulated, the five minutes passed. She had allowed them to pass. His stare had only been broken by his brother's urge towards leaving and her friend's gentle tug on her arm. She had not said goodbye. After he was gone, her senses had gradually come back home, one by one creeping into their places. Her mind took over and within a millisecond of his eyes' departure from her skin, she had written it off as imagination. Even as her friend chattered nonstop about what the look meant, her heart and mind had been working together to protect her from remembering the feeling.

She put down the mug.

Erica Ehrenberg

Destination

Back east
I ask about evangelists
on Sunday morning
but you are no religion
bare foot on the gas pedal
sitting there alone traversing
the American spaces

your mother left with you
when her parents hid her wedding album in the basement
crumbling remnants of a marriage
she cried only when she saw blame
in their tired, red eyes

you must have been behind the Chevrolet window
letting the loud space
slip
wind blowing through your eyes
watching home

your mother silent stirring
coffee with five sugars and four creams
sloshing on the map

you think now remembering
it was that moment when she chose your destination,
the caffeine droplets oozing
past Austin, Texas

you were in the truck stop bathroom adjusting
your white dress with the tiny blue flowers wrinkled
the baby's breath fastened with a pink barrette
loose behind your ear

it is only in the car
you are moving

Rebecca Givens

During This Movie

Here I am at this movie someone said I should watch
and I thought it would be good I guess so that is why
I came   but no one ever mentioned how it would be
so so slow like a droplet down a tree branch or odd
like the faces that droplet reflects   or that I wouldn't
be able to tell if it was drama or comedy   and I'd be so
lost I'd think about other things   like a man I knew once
who never felt in this world   who said he could feel
heavenly anywhere but especially in a movie theater
when he forgets the faces of the people next to him   forgets
their smilings and speech   and ceases to care if the movie
even has a happy ending   then he can shorten his breath
to that of a grasshopper and feel its quick wings tense
feel the brush of its legs as it crumbles some soil   and moves
deep deep inside to beat with the iron core of earth
and the pearl heart of his mother not even buried and
her eyes light   close to him as when he was a child   when
there was one moment of wholeness before the lights are
turned on and the movie ends and he sees himself
clutching an armrest instead of a hand.

Julia Schaffer

Vivian

Vivian is 77 and beginning to wilt.
Like a folded rose, her smell is trailed with a sweet longing
for the end. She envisions the moment when her graceful breath
will fail her. And smooth arms like paths of rain will sail
to her, to hold her and hug her.
Yesterday she visited the dentist. She is telling this to her nephew
Charles, who blinks politely as she speaks.
Her husband's thick hand is fastened around her neck.

"The dentist wore white gloves woven with silk
and tinsel thread. It was only us
in that clean room and a tiny silver tip that brushed
inside my mouth. He held my chin between his fingers
and breathed a minty watery air over my nose and cheek."

"Viv, Charlie ast about your teeth not some doc's breath."

"He hadn't a hair on his face. He ran his pinkie over my gums
like they were lilac petals and he was sniffing carefully so
they wouldn't fall away. I think he was humming...something that
reminded me of the moon and grass as soft as eyelashes.
When he finished he wrapped his arms around my back to lift
me up. I thought I'd float clear to the sky.
There was a sunny bulb to light up my face
as if it were a ballet stage.
He put his fingers against my neck, against my pulse to remind me
of my life."

Vivian moved over to Charles to show him the freckles
over her pulse. But her husband's red thumbprint
had obscured every last one.

"Viv, Charlie ast the name of the operation."

"Oh, oh darling, I don't know the name
but I'm going back for another on Tuesday."

Ryan Hagan

Attire

I remember
the tweed jacket
he wore when drinking
until he was always drinking
and attire became
unimportant.

Ian Kain Amato

Four Haiku

Nora

If my eyes were as bright
as the sun shining off snow
would you look?

Maybe it's simple,
how the sun shines off a leaf,
the last leaf of fall.

Winter Rocks

In winter, on rocks,
I have painted red houses.
The rocks were not changed.

I close my eyelids.
They splash like a water drop
rippling a pond.

Grace Lorentz

Three Poems

Shoes

Old grey shoes lie on the floor
The man who wore them is dead
His feet are ashes sprinkled into a lake somewhere
The woman who knew the man best looks at the shoes
from time to time
She doesn't know whether to give them away
The other things are gone
They remind her of his feet
The bone of the joint before his big toe
The soft skin of the arch
She used to rub them, squeezing with her thumbs
He would smile at her

Watermelon

As a watermelon leaked into a bowl beside us
ferns sprouted from the small of my back
and as your thin arms twined,
flowers blossomed from my navel

Moon

A full blue moon floats in my open mouth
Cupped in pink curves of muscle

I slide my lips around it
And with the tip of my tongue
Explore its salty craters

Nadja Blagojevic

Ode to the Stove

Like the pupils of a cougar
hungry and lean
the stove
snarls softly from the center
of the cabin.

Rusting old,
fired too many winters
by too many city kids
who couldn't start fires,
cleverly designed,
details entwined
on the door,
how odd to find bits of decor on
an item so designed for function.

Double-tiered,
begging
to be used, stretched,
more than heat.
Fry eggs
sauté greens, noodles and garlic.
Tall shiny stovepipe
full of aspirations
and smoke.

Loved by flames,
banisher of chill air,
simple as a flower or a common grass,
defined as an oboe,
haughty and godly.

Ben Patton

Cold Burn

The three fish that Matt carried hung from a short piece of twine looped through their stretched gills and frayed on the gritty teeth of their open jaws. The twine wrapped tightly around the palm of his white hand, which he held as far out from his body as possible. He stood at the top of a sloping forested hill. The patches of bare ground below the trees displayed a collection of plastic bags and aluminum cans that were caked with the decomposing remains of table scraps and leaves. Awkwardly, he threw the dead fish next to a burst water pipe which had been discarded last spring.

Matt scooped up a handful of granular snow and scrubbed his hands. He shook the snow off and stuck his hands in the deep pockets of his thick winter coat before walking back toward the house.

His mom was hunched over the front seat of their flatbed truck when he returned. Fumes of spilled beer and rotting fish rolled out of the truck and hung in the air around the open door. He watched her toss two beer cans into a pile on the snow behind her feet.

She had to do this occasionally. It wasn't right, but she had no choice. If Matt's dad had come out to find the truck smelling as it did and littered with old junk, he would have hit her and yelled that she should clean it up. It didn't matter that it had been him who had made that mess two nights ago when drinking with his friends. Matt's father had come home that night yelling incoherently, waking both Matt and his mother. Neither of them had gotten up, and after an hour of stomping around the house, muttering to himself, he had gone to bed as well.

Since then, Matt and his mother had avoided both the truck and his father. But this morning she had gone straight out and started cleaning. Matt had felt sorry for her and had taken the forgotten fish away. But watching her now, he didn't volunteer for anything else.

"Mom, I'm gonna go over to John's now," he told her. She continued shuffling through the junk in the passenger seat and didn't answer.

Matt turned and walked to the end of their driveway. His hands were warm now along with the rest of his body except for his face, which tingled in the cold air. He could see his breath as he walked down the center of the snow-packed street.

*   *   *   *

"Oh, man. Let's get out of here," John said, slamming the door behind him. "My family drives me crazy."

He paused for the effect, so they could both hear the shouting behind them.

"What's with your sister?" Matt asked.

"She banged up the car on her way home last night."

"Was she drinking again?"

"She must have been, to do what she did to the car. Probably a couple hundred dollars if we ever bother to repair it. But my mom's yelling about her smoking right now."

"I thought you said it was about the car," Matt asked, becoming more interested.

"Well, yeah, I mean it started that way. You know: my mom wakes up and sees the car and gets mad about that and then sees that my sister has a pack of Carltons on her dresser. Then she really gets pissed."

"But your mom smokes too, right?"

"Yeah, our whole house stinks of it. She wouldn't have noticed the smell, but she saw them and off she went. Then she got mad at me, like I had done it too or something. 'If I ever catch you smokin', well, there'll be nothin' to save you from what you got comin',' " he mimicked.

"Jeez. My parents never even bother with talking to me about smoking or drinking or whatever. My mom's too busy dealing with my dad, and my dad doesn't give a shit."

Another road crossed their path, marking the otherwise grey landscape of barren fields and tall twigs of trees at their edges with four bright and useless stop signs. Frost clung to the edges of each, framing the word that was boldly held up by a striped post. Matt fell into single file behind John, and they each gave the post a hard crack with their padded forearms.

About ten feet past the intersection the cement ended but the road continued as gravel to the edge of Little Bob Lake, where Matt and John stopped. A rutted dirt road continued around the lake from there, until turning into the water just next to the Store. The Store was the final destination of most of the locals before heading out onto the lake with their four-wheel drive trucks skidding bravely to their favorite fishing holes.

The Store didn't have a name that anyone knew. You could ask Doug at the counter and he wouldn't know any better than the rest of the town. When Doug bought it the sign above the door had long been destroyed and nobody ever cared to remember what it had said.

Doug's son Alex could be found at the Store most of the time. He'd been a good friend of Matt and John for most of their lives.

Matt kicked a chunk of snow off the ground, uncovering a few flat pieces of cement that were broken up and used for the gravel section of the road. He sidearmed a piece onto the ice where it smacked, accenting the silence that followed, then raced across the flat surface of the lake.

"Are you going to school again once this break is over?" John asked.

"Yeah, I guess so. What else is there to do?"

"I don't know. It just seems kinda' dumb, that's all."

"The girls are there," Matt observed.

"Everyone but Angie." He scraped across her name.

"You're right," Matt smiled, "there's her, if that's what you want."

"I'll leave that to Alex."

There was silence for a moment.

"How long have they been going together?" Matt asked.

"I don't know. It's just disgusting the way they sit tangled together on that dirty old couch while she smokes and he watches dumb cartoons on that little black and white TV they've got. I wonder how many packs of cigarettes he's stolen for her from the Store."

"It must have been since sometime last spring. I know he missed one day of finals. He barely made it to high school with her around."

"Like he's getting anywhere this year."

"Yeah, really. He seems to have decided school isn't for him—"

"And Angie is," John scoffed.

"Hey John! Matt! What are you guys doing here?"

They both turned to see a tall figure hobbling towards them from the path. Hobbling was what Alex did when trying to run. His clumsy legs were too stiff to carry the rest of his bulk at any quick pace. It didn't bother Alex, who rarely thought that where he was going had any importance. Being late only meant wasting another person's time, and so walking suited him quite well.

"Hey, where've you guys been all this time?" Alex asked, catching his breath.

John looked over to Matt, who turned his head towards the lake. "Well, you know, going to school, like normal," John breathed.

John's eyes found the edge of his boot, where the snow had been caught by the stitches that ran between the rubber of the sole and the thick leather that continued up past his ankle. On the inside a layer of coarse wool held the heat in as much as possible. At the center of his shin the grey wool protruded, marking the top of his boot.

"How's Angie?" Matt asked, his eyes still focused away from Alex.

"I guess she's fine. I haven't seen her in a couple weeks," he admitted, then added: "I got tired of having her around."

"What's she doing now?" John asked.

"Oh, I think she went south with some guy from Winona County," he said as he pulled out a bent cigarette from his small coat pocket. He lit it with a Bic that had its child-proof switch torn off. Alex blew a lungful of smoke out in two streams from his nostrils.

It was a cold smoke that Matt smelled. It sat in the air around the three of them, until one of them moved, mixing it with the clear air. When Matt inhaled, the smoke ripped at the flesh in his throat. It tore at one spot below his nose and just above the back of his mouth. It hung there until it had warmed itself comfortably, then sank to rest at the top of his lungs.

Alex took another breath of air to say, "I'm heading back. It's pretty cold out here. If you guys want to tag along I guess you can."

"No thanks," John answered, flipping his words sharply across the air.

Alex looked to Matt briefly, then turned back towards the path. A trail of smoke connected him with the air that hung where he had been.

Matt tossed another stone.

*　　*　　*　　*

The crack of a door stung Matt out of sleep. "...shoved yourself up somebody else's ass!" he heard his father yell.

He heard nothing for a moment after and, when he did, it was the sound of the refrigerator door being opened and slammed shut again.

"...nothing to fuckin' eat around..." His father yelled, crashing out the door to the truck. Matt heard the electric ignition churn for a moment and, when it caught, the engine roared in neutral.

After the headlights passed, it was dark again. It was the darkness of early morning. Matt shoved off his covers and got out of bed. As he dressed, he heard his mom leave through the front door and heard her cracking footsteps on the cold ground. They were quick steps and faded away fast.

After gathering his things for school he grabbed a few slices of bread and a Coke, then left through the front door as well.

The morning was blue with light filtered through the clouds. With the dull white snow and overcast skies, dawn was not a brilliant moment of the sun rising over the crest of a mountain, nor was Matt able to walk into a stream of light where the sun had just reached. A gradual push from the blankness of night brought a blue shade over the trees and the snow at their bases. With time, the light of day arrived, filling the land with a shadowless grey, where it would hold until falling back into darkness that afternoon.

Matt stood by the front steps of the school and ate. When he finished, a teacher who had come to prepare for classes let him in. He flipped through an outdated *Popular Mechanics* in the library until the first bell rang.

Alex wasn't there. He saw John going to classes, but they never spoke. During lunch they ate at different tables, listening to conversations about what others had done over the vacation.

Matt left through the back door the moment his last class was dismissed. As he hurried down the road he saw the buses waiting in front of the school, one of which would have taken him most of the way home. His boots chewed the snow, lifting imprints and dropping them with his next step.

He stopped when he had arrived at the Store.

Filtered through walls, the blaring orchestra of cartoons drifted out towards Matt. He opened the door and was hit with the full sound and thick musty smell from inside.

"Alex?" Matt yelled.

"Hey! How're you doing?" Alex looked up from a pile of lures that he was shuffling through.

"Fine."

"Let me grab my coat." After a moment Alex hobbled outside to the porch with Matt.

"You weren't busy, were you?" Matt asked.

"Oh, don't worry about it. I was just sorting out some new fishing junk for the store, but it's no problem." They walked down the small trail to the edge of the lake. "How was school?"

"Fine, I guess."

"Oh? I never found it even that interesting." He pulled out a pack of Marlboro cigarettes, and lit one for himself.

"Do you want one?" Alex added, seeing Matt watch him.

The words were hard to get out, though his decision had been made hours before. "Yeah, okay."

Matt fingered one out of the pack. The white wrapping was smooth and even. The feeling helped to relax his nervous hand. Alex flicked his lighter. It took a moment for the cigarette to catch.

The filter was warm touching his lips, but the smoke burned. It burned the back of his mouth and throat. He flung the burning smoke from his mouth with a cough and soothed the pain with saliva.

As he inhaled again the burning was less, and the smoke was warm in his lungs.

Both Alex and Matt turned at the sound of someone behind them. John stood in observance with his backpack still on. He looked to Matt, who quickly turned away.

"Hi. "

"Hey," Alex replied.

John walked over to Matt. "Go ahead, don't bother about me."

The smoke twisted inside as Matt took another pull. His eyes fixed on the ice in front of him.

John looked over to Alex. "Got another one?"

"Uh, yeah, just a second." He fumbled with one hand to get the pack out of his pocket. He thumbed the edge of a cigarette out towards John, who took it smoothly.

They all had lit cigarettes, and when John stopped coughing they stood together in warmth. The air around them was unmoving and protective from the cold when they stood still. The smoke warmed them from inside as well, with more than the heat from the flame.

Alex's throat was numb. For John and Matt, it burned.

Erin Beach

Poulsbo

On Highway 305 the busy street
shines like a wet seal.
With their trash-picker-uppers, road crew members
collect trash as the mud slithers under their feet.
The Washington Babe Ruth Champions reside here and
I wonder if I were seven again, could I hit a fly ball once more,
but as it is, I am too old, and so I can't.
A boy called Dan emphasized full gas
houses in June. Why? No one knows.
The dry rain kept the boy from bullying another
and the raspy laugh echoed like a mountain.
As mayor of Poulsbo I would establish an ordinance
that disallows rainfall within city limits.
The Chevron gas station was once
a sewer dumpage.
And now the Babe Ruth losers cry themselves
to sleep. The hot ice falls to the ground softly.
To be a cow in Poulsbo is to be normal.
For a good time call 598-0989, and the
smell of salt water reminds me that this is home.
The waiter in Azteca Restaurant couldn't speak English and
so we made fun of him. He agreed.
Where would Christopher Robin shop? At Coast
to Coast? I wouldn't know. All I know is
that the road looks like a wet seal.

Christopher Lew

Faculty Christmas Party
at Webster Middle School

Mr. Davids, 7th Grade English, stands before the bowl of nachos,
His head bopping to the Grateful Dead.

Mrs. Chan, Music, sits at the table by the door. The one
James Haskins calls the wussy table.

Mr. Williams, Woodshop, pushes open the swinging door. Back
From the main office where Sarah Lupkin jammed her bloody nose
        with tissues.

Mrs. Kilowski-Smith, just married, doesn't attend,
Left yesterday for Barcelona.

Mr. Palmer, Earth Science, has his arm on the back
        of Mrs. Chan's chair.
His eyes wander over Ms. Samson's reindeer sweater.

Ms. Samson, 6th Grade Math, can't believe there's
        four shopping days
Left, wants to get an ab-roller for her brother in Kalamazoo.

Ms. Fessel, Gym, is still in her sweatpants. Jimmy "the Rat" Nissen
Said he saw her in his brother's porno mag.

Mrs. Bonn, Art, is driving up to New York City
Tomorrow to see the tree and her sister.

Mr. Taylor, 7th Grade Biology, pops in to grab a Coke
Before heading home to catch the Simpsons rerun.

Mr. Libowitz, 8th Grade English, wants to get crazy drunk.
Forget Christmas, New Year's is coming.

Karen Emmerich

Perception

A boat slides
along the horizon,
slow and large as all
Portugal pulled long,
prow to stern.

To those on shore it is
nothing, less even
than absence—the waves
recede into themselves
clear and unbroken, lapping
against no miraculous steel.

What is there now
is replaced by what has
always been there—a child
spins a round flat stone
into the froth, and how
quickly the sea recovers.

Samara Adsit Holtz

Field

Wind moved through
the field like flood
water. It split the pale
stalks; it came between.

That day
the sun came down, hovered
just above the flat
land. Grass blew against
it, brittle and even.

Matthew Joy

Outcrop

red-tinged rock outcrop
a face of blue-gray lichen
containing mysteries
known only to the dead buffalo
driven by the Dakota
onto a cool, calm lake
of green grass and yellow flowers
while the sky watches
through millions of years
recording these secrets

Matthew Joy

A Poem in the Wave

beams of sunlight
penetrate clouds
oil rigs stare
water circling with wind
pounding, slapping
a dead sea gull
and a curious piece of metal
kaleidoscope of fascinations
from the sea

Matthew Joy

Residential Whiskey in Hand

foggy cobbles under heavy waders
banks' white windows closed
Irish eyes in the mist
somewhere people are—
lonely street with its only friend
leads to the valley Wye
only color sun paint overhead

Matthew Joy

Morning Run

oak pine oak
a grayness in my eyes
two deer on a hill
smelling the acorn
while I breathe by

Alexis Goldberg

The Bicyclers

I saw them today, two of them, seven to nine, I'd venture to guess
Off on a wild adventure
Faster than anything they were flying the two of them one
      behind the other
And then
The other behind one
Up and down and up and down and everywhere around
      the driveway they flew
Until you knew that they couldn't possibly really be in the driveway
Going at that speed
That they must be somewhere else
Off somewhere bicycling their lungs out in some grand prix
Racing, racing
Racing to win, winning to race, going for win
Faster and faster and all of a sudden it's dark, and time to go inside
(and time to go inside)
And it's time to go inside
So they abandon the race and wheel home, putting their
      medals into the trophy case,
In the attic with all the rest.

Shayna Strom

Schuylkill Valley Park

Willows weep
at the pool,
washing their hair
in the cracked mirror
when the bullet comes.

When the bullet comes,
the withered brown park bench,
empty and peeling,
open to everyone,
is already cold.

White cotton cloud
bustles up through sky
unraveling like a loose thread
to hide in the corner, fading
in air
that the bullet tears.

So the swing
empties itself
of the little girl
and the grass lies
smoldering
and quivers in shock
as if the mower
had just passed.

Beth Kinderman

Casey

She hasn't said three words to me yet.
She bows her head to rest in hands
pale and smooth, closes eyes
that seem to have spent years awake.
I watch the halo of her hair,
a cloud of chaff around her shoulders,
follow the paths of capillaries,
purple rivers just beneath wax paper skin.

There's nothing I can do
to help her today.

At last we set aside third grade math,
go separate ways without goodbyes.
As I leave I glimpse her by the door,
standing tiptoe on a cracked plastic chair,
her whole body stretched toward the ceiling lights,
poised and hollow, not ready to fly.

II
A Wing in My Mouth

William Lopez

Lemonade

There is a wing in my mouth;
it is flapping.
It is not my tongue, it is not
a bird's wing, a bird's tongue;
it is the wing of a whip,
the detail of a spark, the tip,
the taking-notice.

The end of a poem
always catches
the eye.

Christopher Lew

Missile

There was a crash and an explosion,
said the reporter in Iraq. No one cared.
Linda Reed lay backwards on the couch
with her feet over the back, her ass
in the air, breasts pressed into the seat cushion,
and her elbow bent into my knee
as she tried to suck down the last of the Sam Adams.
Steve Anderson was breathing through his mouth
holding an empty bottle as Laura Bates and Jessica Larson
giggled and raced to take off their bras
with their tops still on. Danny Chu pushed me over
and sat down on the couch. Linda's ass
was next to my head. The brown stitching
on the rear pockets looped once and arced
across. I wanted to slap it.
On television a burnt missile lay half buried
in the ground like the Zinfandel bottle
I found on the beach.

Han-Yeh Katharine Lo

Journey

A proud trumpet slices through the air. I turn left onto Foothill Expressway. The late afternoon sun envelops me. I hear a sound and turn my head. He walks up to me. He does not stop at *to me* though. He holds the note one-sixteenth too long. The rays flicker intermittently through the trees lining the left median. He leans into the quarter-note rest. The pine tops outline a uniformly jagged ridge. The sharp *tatatata-le* of the snare drum announces the clarinet solo. I hear the drawn-out note growing and expanding into a blaring color. The light glares red. I press down on my angled right. He makes me uneasy. The car slows and abruptly stops just over the white line. Striding across the carpeted floor, which dulls the authority of his steps, he asks, civilly, *Where were you?* He inches forward. *No! No!* The conductor drops her arms. *You must have power. Keep bow near bridge. Like this.* The bow hits the strings. The tension explodes. I cannot see her. The horizontal rays blind me at the zenith. I roll over the asphalt hill and meet a cold shadow. I rush down with terrible speed. My fingers fly, descending the scale, and I resolve the phrase for one, four-beat whole note. *1. 2. 3....* The hazy, haloed yellow measure finishes in discordant red. Doesn't he see? Doesn't he hear? The score says C natural. He played C sharp and made it minor. Green silences the dissonance. I rise up. The asphalt rolls under me. The beat quickens. The ridged pines *tatatata-le*. He cannot hear it. He cannot see it. *I thought you might have left.* Without him. The red light bars the road. In the distance, the sun cuts a wide swath across a shadowless stretch. The snare speeds past. The warm flows through the window onto my cheek. I flush. The line soars higher and higher. I struggle to sustain G. French horns support with an anchored C. The cellos, pines lining the left median, stand the middle ground, *E*. A major chord. I turn right. Towards home.

David Konieczkowski

East Jordan

When my father would fly out of Hopkins Airport with me sitting copilot in his single-engine Bonanza, he would look out the window after he cleared the runway and point down at the railroad tracks. David, he would say, out there is where the railroad is. Out there are the railroad tracks and you see them going into the IX Center that used to be a bomber plant in World War II and a tank plant before that. Now there are shows there sometimes and carnivals, and inside I have walked around the cement floor and seen in the cracked gray concrete and the brown metal beams high overhead the Shermans and B-24s and B-29s that were made across this floor. I have seen out the open sliding metal doors made to let out the bombers, looking out the doors because there are no windows, the railroad tracks that slide off through weeds and gravel through barbed wire fence to the airport before they stop, the old orange-brown of iron dripping into the sandy earth and the dirty green of weeds growing. I remember how the rails V'd apart and one track headed off south to Berea and the other north into Hopkins. I remember crawling down those tracks to the airport when I was eight and small, with jets screaming above me and air lapping at their wings in the summer heat. I remember feeling the breath of their engines in front of the fence and black on white "No Trespassing" signs, seeing the writing raised on the rails, "85 pounds per rail foot—East Jordan Iron Works—East Jordan, Michigan," following the tracks all the way to the barbed wire before I had to stop. I remember the fence there that was covered in thin gray metal strips so you couldn't see into the airport—my father said this was to keep drivers on the Berea Freeway from being distracted. I remember crawling back up the tracks to the IX center and then south along the other pair of tracks and getting a few hundred yards away, seeing the old ties rotting away into the rocks they sat on and I remember my father saying to me from the pilot's seat, David, those tracks are old and here we soar above them.

Jeffrey Chiu

Considerations

1.
"Let's sit under that tree," suggests Joe.
That's as specific as it ever gets.
We know maples, evergreens, apple trees
by sight. He can recognize elms
and sycamores. Nevertheless we walk over
and settle down in the shade under a cover
of anonymous branches and leaves.

2.
We're eating hamburgers, and he's telling me
about the dream he had last night,
where he helped extinguish a fire in his apartment
and saved many people. Then his friend
from next door came to him, holding the burnt body
of a small dog. "What does it mean?" I ask.
He looks into his soda and says only that it was sad.

3.
The field guide contains photographs
and descriptions of a thousand varieties
of trees. I read about their height,
size of leaves, color, texture of bark;
easily identifiable traits. I'm thinking
the next time I step outside, I will look
at the neighbor's tree and still feel clueless.

4.
"You need to learn to relax," he says
after a period of my usual quiet.
We are browsing baseball caps in a store.
I bring attention to the ones that beg
to be noticed for their ugliness.
He points to a cap on the third row
and says it's the nicest one. I silently agree.

5.
I have given up on trying to name the trees.
Everyone is predicting snow for tonight,
enough to layer over and silence the dead leaves
rolling noisily across the road. Tomorrow
morning I want to wake up, go to the window,
see only white and hear nothing. I want to know
that what is nameless will always exist.

Anna Soo-Hoo

Pineapple Days of Sunshine

Ai caramba! It's so hot!
Where's my yellow polka dot bikini?
(rummage, rummage....)
There are glitters of a
saffron color—pats of natural
warmth on the head, on shoulders.
I say a golden disposition
doth beget riches and glory. Riches
of an intangible sort, I mean.
Anyway, it's the laughter
that I hear in the fields of corn.
The peewee kernels all giggle
with fun as they give spurts of
growth from time to time. And corn
husks near burst with hearty laughs
with all this tickling going on.
Look at her go with that tango.
Hmph. Give me a piña colada—
more frutas, less rum—and I'll
dance it with more sass than that.
But have a lemon, luv.
Say "lollipop" for me.
Luscious, luscious life:
wouldst thou always be so good to me.
With a snap of attitude,
it's "Honey, don't push your luck."

Julie Scharper

The Beginning

of spring—wild
geese wake
me at four a.m.
Migrating, their wet

calls first sound
like someone opening
drawers in another
room. They pull

me from my bed but
from this window I
can see nothing;
it is night. This

changes everything.

Jessica Bulman

Revelation

It was not the place
for a revelation
not the time or the place
crammed into
the sweating locker room
heavy heat and stale humidity
clinging to rust
clinging to desiccated
showerheads
and to darkness
shade pouring from
grey lockers in lines
locks screaming
voices banging into metal

And then
from the one high window
a sliced sheet of light
plastered itself to me
and stuck
voices spun themselves
into silence
last lock clicked
perfectly
on its combination
and my face was shrouded
in a jab of light

But it was not the place
for a revelation
a mass of grey
concealed the sun
my hand dug out a cleat
bottom mud-stained
and grass-filled
my watch whined
and the voices
remembered to clash

Rebecca Givens

I Lose Constellations in Foreign Cities

I lose constellations in foreign cities
a few degrees displacement, and Orion has
turned, rotating his sword haphazardly
in the star-trance milk of night. He
is fighting a new battle now

with Cassandra, priestess now of
a place as well as time which has no
need for her braids, her voice
echoing of a city I do not remember

which my skin knows, hanging loosely
around as if a few organs had been
removed, lost in the speedy motion
of unthinkably high air....

Cloudy tonight. My star charts wail
their final uselessness—inept soldiers,
prophets of one latitude only who
lose Polaris among a million stars.

Foreignness makes my heart's heel
homesick for hearths of flaming figures,
the single spot of back yard. Where
have you gone, smooth atrial flow,
you map laid of true-blood stars?

Rebecca Givens

The End of Our Manifest Destinies

This land of course was once like a galaxy,
freckled and unexplored. We met it as
tourists would, accidentally, calling the
wrong names. *New, new!* we yelled to
those already living here, dusky with pale
comets of hair. Reaping the spoils of
buffalo and land, we carved necklaces,
left waste by the road. We came to this
new land and prospered, multiplied,
were fruitful, crowded each other in.

Then we staked our claim: west was our
New World—it was where the sun went
after a long day's work. We could come
too, clear and orange-warm, biting into
small suns with our teeth. Unhurried and
open, we could corral our hearts out to
the nearest fence post. But soon we heard
this new land was too much like our own:
landlessness by the thin springs, gamblers,
some years of drought, then debts.

We holed up in our crisp facilities then,
straining under hot lights and the burden
of watching closely. There must be a new
kind of gasoline, a fuel to set us far. Take
a billion tons of fire, and we'll shoot off
to space, limber inside dust spots near the
moon. Gravity in our ships is nothing,
we calculated; you fly around freely and
whole. Only a black strap (you hardly
notice) connects you to the consoles.

We never really thought if the cord were
to split, if we happened to break from our
plastic homes....It would be like something
from a bad science fiction movie, as if
Columbus had never found land. We

would simply speed to the edge of the
world and back, wandering, leaving no
star unexplored. Only our hearts would
sound a new awakening in our shuttles,
our eyes brisk with fear's milky ways.

Emma Straub

Bliss

These shit-covered lakes, empty driving ranges
these closed bus windows, these

all reek of bliss in mid aft
late September—Somber skies

warn of inherent gloom and
off tomatoes weaken constant motion.

And yet, bliss—Moving between
New London and Providence a

happy medium is rediscovered ,
a love for speed renewed, ground

covered over distance traveled
divided by hours taken equals here—

loving exquisite time alone, on the road
even better, god bless planes and buses and
government-supported locomotion through
the vast countryside, who ever saw so many
leaves, so many fields of pussy willows
and sunflowers? Contemplative hours
in transit, splayed again against
patterned seat covers, nearly licking
the bulletproof plexiglass for want
of security in this situation, a promise
of more highways to come—

Strike me down now if this isn't perfectly lovely.

Matthew Moses

This Day Was a Poem

Even before I got to your house
I knew this day was to become a poem.

*

I took notes as I walked to you:
the sun was wet from a rain
but shining on crumbly streets.
In the bowels of Brooklyn, where we live,
the damp is never flattering—
it brings out the dirt
and the lonely flecks of broken gray concrete.

I was wearing sunglasses,
and it was fall.
People rarely wear sunglasses in fall.
I rarely wear them even in summer.

On the edge of the park
the leaves were matted
into a green-brown mess;
the rain must've taken them down.
I didn't even realize it had been raining
until I left the house.
It was obvious, though,
you could see it was a quick downpour.
Sometimes you don't even realize
those things are happening.

But eventually you notice
when you see the matted leaves
sticking to the black,
and the weighted trees drip
fat lima bean drops
on your head and neck
and the gutters are dense
with mush and thick water
that just won't drain.

As I got closer to your house
the rain became more noticeable
my feet slipped on the big avenues with no cars.
The cars that did pass—
dusty Dodges that the rain only made dirtier—
spat at me.

*   *   *   *

When I came home
dry patches were showing up,
the leaves were starting to blow again;
the drops had stopped.

                    *

This day was a poem.
I wish it was less than that,
            but it was more.

Lauren Brozovich

The Original Gaither Farmhouse

—Ellicott City, Maryland

The tartness of fruit is gathered
in the woodwork: sour cherries, seedless
grapes, mouthfuls of white plum. The wall
panels pulsate with sap sugar, pectin,
and the lost potential of making paper. The wains-
coting boasts fruit at furniture, inherited
wood frames buttoned with plush,
damask, wood-ringed moire. The porcelain
dishes everywhere set down in tea rings
smell of nuts. Printed with frosting-soft
flowers, they smell pastel
as sucked-on Jordan almonds.

Pastel Cadillacs flooding the driveway
like dish-mints. Ice cream
shutters. Cedar siding. Lent-out
garden plots of corn and gladioluses. Large
bulb Christmas lights. Old-fashioned
two-piece telephones. Prune faces. Peach
pits tongued wryly in cheeks. Fruit-
colored croquet sets. Cushions
crimped with cherry pits, just so.

The year the cicadas
crawled out of the earth-holes
thick as locusts, there was truth. With their
multitudes of litmus red & blue
eyes, they threatened the cushion
buttons, the window seats, the Limoges breakfast
bowls, the pegged floors, and
the Neapolitan chalk portrait of their only
child, Anne, the demure
blonde-drawn girl above the mantel
who left their Maryland farm
replete with race horses, barns, graves
because she loved TEXAS!

Even the gladioluses must have been crawling
with cicadas that year. In later years,
when old age brought on neglect, I would be given
them, fresh-cut in buckets
that could not be brought into the house
because they were crawling with ants.
Even the corn that was brought into the house
leaked clear worms into our water pots.

I came the summer they came, 1987.
I was seventeen at Gaither Farm.
I respected the cicadas' claims
to longevity. They swarmed
as thick above ground as the 17th-century
graves beneath ground. They pulled
primary color beads over the pastel scrim-
med portrait of Anne. Uncountable,
they covered finite plots
of earth, picture frames, preserve
jars, bridge dishes,

headstones, footstones.
The cicadas only come once
every seventeen years. With planetary precision,
they and their patriotic Rocket Pop eyes
crawl out of Maryland soil and woodwork
making cherry pit patterns over the earth
until the land is thick with them.

Lauren Brozovich

The Pistachio Dress

It was pistachio
green like Lady Bird
Johnson's inaugural gown
only hers had the sexy covered
zipper with the mint tongue
that dangled between her breasts
and didn't zip to cover
a V of decolletage, collar
bones, and neck flesh. Even
comparing the two on
mannequins, you could tell
that hers with that sexy zipper
was more risqué. Mine had
a placket of buttons—
modest ones sewn down
the whole front of the dress. It was Laura
Ashley, almost eighteenth
century-looking, with long
panels of silk printed with periwinkles
and a seven-inch flounce
that grazed the ankle. I could
only wear it on special occasions
because it wrinkled terribly. The
silk would twist in
sections like withering
gladiolus blooms, all sweat and
spiralling fibers. It had to be
dry-cleaned. After touring the First Ladies
exhibit in the Smithsonian
Museum of American History and
having a forty-year-old man
put his feet in between my
feet until I was pressed
against the glass in front of Mamie
Eisenhower's punch-red gown,
I wore it to the awards
ceremony. I walked
into the Corcoran Gallery of Art

and someone commented that
the color reminded them of pistachio ice
cream, or Lady Bird
Johnson's inaugural gown. I thought of
my buttoned buttons compared to
that impossible zipper. I thought
of the time this modest watercolor
dress made my boyfriend unable
to calm down: in the basement,
after dinner, when I slipped
it off so it wouldn't wrinkle
and draped it over the ottoman—limpid,
hollow, not sweat-soaked, *in the absence
of all desire* like Daisy
Buchanan's balloon-white dresses
or Abigail Adams' inaugural
gown in the Smithsonian,
which is displayed flat
on a table in a climate-controlled case
under low-level lighting
to preserve the fabric. I don't
quite understand
the effect of the preservation
of fabric on men.

Erica Ehrenberg

Montana Storm

When the first lightning struck
distances away
the fire of another space
I knew
as the Cheyenne knew
what was to come

I had thought that it was their spirits
whispering the sky's intentions
before I saw the approaching clouds myself
blast cracking through the biggest sky

she would come to see the rain
I closed my eyes and waited
my back pressed to the white stucco building
crowned with a cross
bent like a rooster weather vane
forgotten on a crumbling roof

the children's dark eyes lifted
holding their hands out to the air
crunching the wet gravel with their bare feet
raindrops like fingertips on their faces
I skimmed my hands through puddles
forming around me the color of nymphs

but her palm was closed
I thought of her brother's tumor
only spiritual doctors on the rez
she eats canned American beans
frost-caked Ore-Ida French fries from the bag
when mother is locked behind doors
sick from drinking
but cupped inside her hand was a sparrow
she found drowning
wet and silent she wanted me to tell her
he would live

Nadja Blagojevic

After Rumi

Have you seen the girl?
Hands like sparrows, perfect pitch, capricious eyes.
Long, long reaching arms.

Presses secrets into the palm of your hand,
wonderful and gnarled, like fish.

Strong voice, solemn nose,
always lying.

Elusive as a handful of elvers
she can climb a tree in the dark,
and tango madly with her eyes shut.

We search for her unconsciously,
spurred on by innate tendencies.
We want nothing more than a glance, and
a few wise words.

William Lopez

Amy

Amy is a tiny woman,
every part is small,
voice soft and small,
small like a dollhouse is
in proper proportion.

Rides the train down
to Chinatown, walks short steps, and
mashed between the busy Chinese people
is a pinball: what
moves your eyes,
makes your fingers twitch,
makes you careful to be quick.

The ring glinting off
the finger of your beloved,
winking kisses in high, cold breath.

A speck of glittery diamond dust;
a fragment of bone
and a piece of glass.
            When she speaks, she sparkles.
Beauty quivering,
skin moves fast,
hair shivers.

Too mini to be missed,
and we are all desirous.

Later on in life,
blush within,
envying your little boy
for a fiery leaf he found.
Know why he likes it.

Matthew Moses

Two-Dollar Bills

when you had to sit
on the hall steps to read
mother—peeling carrots
siblings—dirty carrot peel fight
you—called in
named discipline
too many children
and you were the oldest,
born 1911

mother — you quit your job
          at the telephone company
          when she died
siblings — one is dead now
          the other you
          refuse to speak with
          and refer to as the *maître' d*
          the others were boys
          your father could handle them
          and the baby,
          she's sixty-seven now,
          you still call her that—
          the baby.

discipline (you) —
          all the beds used to
          have high legs back then
          you could hide anything
          under them
          plump little girl legs
          were there the day after
          the funeral
          the *maître' d* whispered to
          the baby as you looked for them
          "don't worry we don't have
          to listen to her,
          she's not our mother."
          you, like the Pope who visits now
          had to wield a staff—
          a violent shepherd
          with a broomstick.

violent shepherd (discipline (you)) —
                    the papal visit
                    is exciting for you
                    wishing you could be there,
                    in Central Park
                    remembering Latin prayers
                    at least you know
                    what they mean now
                    the new church in your
                    retirement community
                    doesn't serve
                    Reconciliation (forgiveness)
                    the priest you asked
                    told you just to pray
                    maybe he didn't want you
                    to come out in the new weather—
                    fall (are you?)

fall (violent shepherd (discipline (you)))—
                    your Hungarian husband
                    never lost his accent
                    He was actually born here,
                    One Hundred and Twelfth Street,
                    before Harlem was colored—
                    you don't say it with malice,
                    it's just a fact
                    like your swollen feet
                    and doctors who don't know anything
                    and try to drug you up
                    and you had to wait
                    two hours for a cab home
                    from the mini-mall yesterday
                    and you never were able
                    to have children
                    and you are waiting to die now
                    and the two-dollar bills
                    you remember and promise
                    to give me.
                    they'd at least be nice to see,
                    they've been discontinued
                    they're a piece of history now.

Michael Mirer

The Revolution Will Not Be Televised

"My man Gil Scott-Heron once said: ' The revolution will not be televised.'"
—D-Knowledge

The revolution began on Sunday at 7/6 Central. *60 Minutes* was on. Maine and Vermont didn't have a chance. The rebels had been holed up in Canada for weeks, and made the first advance. When it was 6 in the Mountain time zone, they took Montana. Alaska was the last to fall on Sunday. CBS heard a call from their affiliate in Portland, but wouldn't interrupt their news show.

No one reported the revolution, so it took Monday off.

Tuesday began with reports of unnamed problems in the Northeast and Northwest. The affiliates couldn't be reached to confirm or deny the stories. None of the networks went with it as a lead story on their morning shows. NBC didn't mention it at all. The *Today* show was devoted to a corruption scandal in the White House kitchen.

The revolution made small gains on Tuesday night during *Must See TV*. The revolution secured the entire American-Canadian border, and took New Hampshire and Massachusetts. There were no reports of any kind.

The revolution took Wednesday off.

Thursday was a massacre.

When *Friends* began at 8/7 Central, the revolution took over the rest of New England, New York City, Detroit, Chicago, Milwaukee, and Minneapolis. The revolution's planners made sure that no one interfered with the television signals. No one took notice that the cities were under new leadership. Everyone sat in front of the television. *Friends* was good that night. Ross and Rachel nearly broke up, Joey and Phoebe went to Bloomingdale's and stole a sweater, and Chandler pretended to be Monica's husband for a job interview.

By the time Jerry Seinfeld appeared on America's television sets, most of the north half of the country had been taken. There was no body count to the revolution. *Seinfeld* wasn't anything special, but still drew a twenty rating that night. The entire eastern seaboard was taken by the commercial break, and the revolution began to march west. NBC New Orleans got hold of the story, and was going to break in, but decided to hold off until the end of *Seinfeld*. The station was taken before they could broadcast a warning.

They took the White House during *Suddenly Susan.*

When *ER* ended on Thursday night at 11 Pacific time, the entire United States was in the hands of the revolution. The news anchors read scripts on the late news. The American people were told that the president was no longer in control, and that the revolution was there to rebuild America the way it was when it was founded. Most of the people didn't watch the news. They flipped to *Night Court* or *Cheers* or whatever was on in syndication against the local news.

On Friday, an eight o'clock curfew was imposed, and the phone lines were cut at nine. Everyone watched *Millenium.* Those foolish enough to defy the revolution were taken prisoner, and disappeared. The leader of the revolution went on Letterman that night, bumping Jack Nicholson back to Monday. Leno won in the ratings that night. The revolution declared itself victorious, and no one cared.

The revolution was in complete control when they took Saturday off.

There's nothing to watch on Saturday.

Ben Lerner

Big Bang

> *A group of fourth graders in Texas was instructed to glue shut the two pages of their science book that offered a non-creationist theory on the origin of the universe*
> —*The Progressive* Magazine

A fourth grader
touches the sticky stuff of creation
in the bubbles formed
by an excess of glue

And peels back a page far enough
to see the words
Big Bang
written in block letters

Later at recess
hiding behind the sandbox
he mouths the words like a sacred obscenity
"cock. . . pussy. . . Big Bang."

David Konieczkowski

There Is Water Here That Burns

Jesus rode into Cleveland once in the diesel room of an ore boat that came in from the lake five miles north. He screamed in the ear of the engineer over the roar of the engines, I am coming to Cleveland because there is water here that burns. The engineer nodded in his overalls torn with rust and looked back to the engines abusing the air with their pistons moving in and out down by Jesus' robes that flew up around his legs. Jesus came out of the engine room when the ship was wedded to the old concrete pier that thrust out into the lake and scared children who were swimming farther to the west at the rich suburban beaches. He walked up out of the engine room on the metal grating that pressed into his skin and bones, feeling the air from the pistons biting at his robes before he shut the bulkhead door and threw the latch closed. Jesus came ashore by the old Conrail cargo cranes rusting at the lakeshore, the ones the mayor always wanted to be destroyed because, he said, they were too ugly next to the cement breakwall with foam crashing over it, the seagulls roosting on it between the waves. He walked down by the cranes' rusty crossed foundations that stained the cement brown, flakes of rusted iron snowflaking down onto his hair, manna in a desert browned with heat. Jesus did not go down by the part of the river down by the new-cut mouth, with the paved cement and tiles shining bright in the sun, because it looked like the floor of St. Peter's dripping slowly down into the river. Jesus went east and then south down to the stretch of the river that is the color of the grit on top of the steel mills' smokestacks—he went there and walked out on the water, oily with rainbows that smelled of sulfur from the mills. And with the waves flaming around his robes, Jesus kept on walking and watched as the seagulls flew up and away from him, burning the color of sunsets.

Mike Livshits

Ma Melts Things, Has an Orgasm

Ma takes the soldering iron by the
Power cord. She swings it in
Arcs that melt the living room.
When there is no more living room,
She walks across the front lawn
And gets on a pink bicycle
With a long hard seat. She pedals
To Corp Co. Headquarters, 87th floor.
Board of Directors: eight men, three women.
Swoosh hwoosh says the soldering
Iron, melting men, and their dicks
Flutter to the floor.
8 men   7 men
6 men   5 men
4 men   3 men   2 men

Two men look at three untouched
Women, the five resume voting on
Bottom lines, human lives,
Splitting stock, putting debtors
Under lock and key for nonpayment....
Ma melts a door in the wall next to
The corporate logo, she walks through
The air eighty-seven floors up, she melts
The glass ceiling, just keeps on rising....

Later, in an apartment looking over
Washington Square Park, Ma crumbles
Beneath Justina's moist fingers, after being
Mishandled by men for eighteen years,
Her first orgasm....

Quentin Rowan

Prometheus at Coney Island

Up over the swell of hot sugar
up over the swell of rubber
Up over the death creaks, rises and falls
like heart attacks
Up over the backyards and bricks
Up over the smell of Ms. Roha's beans
Up over fat men in boxer shorts
Up over the people in ticket stands
Who hate you.
Up over the haunted houses and
1942 ectoplasm.
Up over the Coney Island gray beach,
over the Coney Island gray water that will
make your shins itch.
Up and turning,
circling back over the city, back over pipes
and billboards, pressures and nausea;
our car turns and sways and equilibriums
like greased jets and leather.
Over the swell of hot sugar at Coney Island
they pulled him hard,
under a yellow snow-line:
gesticulating without talking,
creaking like the shingles of an ancient house,
raising and lowering like breath
sighing farewell to its ancient patriarch
blowing kisses as he's taken away,
like a famed entertainer heaving in the public eye.
                In the impaling sun
they threw him into the sea of
Pomatum grease,
                to singe his beard and
rid him of his dirt.
                Watermelons and pumpkins
were brought, and a pipe of brass to keep cool
his face—so as to show sick
newborn smartness,
                an avatar

of polka dancers.
        And laid out was an accordion
and Pannish mouth harp
under which clasped women could dance in the
sand—
moaning over containers overrun with fruit and fish.
Under the figure eights of gulls—
decorating the sand's own dead hills,
lighting fire in the company of thrills,
as was life in the old country.

Olivia Ophelia Harman

High Way

Plain talk he said
and she nodded
not meaning it
and he laughed and slid
lower towards the steering wheel—
that's crazy she said
we're not even in a car
and he picked up
a strand of her hair—
red—
and wrapped it
lazily
around his whole hand
and she said
that's stupid
I cut my hair and bleached it
you never look at me
He glanced in the rearview mirror
and gassed the pedal,
merging lanes.

Erin Hoover

So Natural

In the NYU dorm,
students are throwing
their heads back.
It is his first time,
and Stephanie helps him
with a pale hand.
The cocaine, wet
against the back
of his throat, rolls
thick mucus
back to his brain
and the headache starts.
His eyes swell,
he is dizzy.
This girl and this powder,
this is New York,
he thinks, running
his slender hands
over the creases of his leather
pants. Stephanie holds
her cigarette like it
is just another one
of her white fingers,
so natural, she knows it.
The two laugh
at their friends stooping
over the mirror,
and he gloats to know
he looks the same,
his nose
as smudged and chalky
as theirs, his head
bent back
even farther.

Gemma Cooper-Novack

As the Child Prodigy Grows Up

he wonders about his children:

wonders what
he'll do when
one of them can't figure out
a spelling test

when his daughter
is confused by
chemistry & algebra
overwhelms
his son

he wonders if he
will be able
to help them or if
he will expect them to understand
everything,

(the eight-year-old who took calculus, physics and honors English
swore before a class of seniors that he'd never have children
but that was before he knew
her, before he discovered the longing)

he fears the father
he will become:
worse than the
one who does not
appreciate intelligence is
the one who
cannot appreciate
those who lack it

and he wonders
if he will
desert
the ones he should love

because they won't
understand the
words he
uses to say "I love you."

*

She knows the man she loves
is smarter than she is, that she learns things today
that he knew when he was twelve, but has no objection:
he will teach her, and they'll have kids
who will be smart, smarter than she was
when she was younger.
She's smart enough for him to love her, anyway.
The only thing that worries her
is night: when he touches her
when they slip into sex, will it matter
to him, or will he break her into anatomy?
Can he possibly slide from the scientific
to the sensual
or will words like copulation,
reproduction, intercourse, impregnation,
conjugation, procreation,
parturition, fructification, parturience, conception,
commerce, fertilization, consummation
rest on his lips
at the moment of climax
instead of her name?

William Lopez

Brambles

Rough brambles in the yard
bleed back black berry blood,
unnoticed by the pushing man
shoving through the brambles, rough
and veteran.

Sarah Nooter

The Way She Burned

He caught her by a sleeve,
the way doorknobs had before.
His tongue licked
the pale baby bottom of
her wrist and he
sucked on her fingers.
He bit off her fingernails.

It was later than dusk; the
gray dust of the sinking
sun had melted into darkness.
It was dark.
She fried tomato slices
with parsley and she poured
hungry, virgin olive oil
all over her tomato meat.
The oil slid over the slick
red bodies and then danced
around in the pan. It danced,
angry, excited and it sent
tiny tongues, tiny babies
out into the world: one
bit her chin, another
tasted her eye.
When she had finished cooking,
a plate was drinking the
essence and color of
ripe tomato and she was
soaking the weary pan
in tap water. She turned
to her whispering meat.
Tomato smiled
at her, and blew hot,
sweet kisses to her.

And when she was walking over
to her steaming reward
he caught her by the
sleeve; his hand was

black and iron. He
caught her with just
one finger, a finger
that knew the screams
of fire like no one
else. He caught her
and kissed her
all over.

The dark darkened
and the burner
burned and
kept burning.

III
Tell Them It's a Potato

Julie Scharper

Rain

"Tell them it's a potato,"
my best friend suggests. Or I could say
it is her voice, her words hitting me in cold
droplets that warm as they run down my back.
Which is already wet with school's
downpour: long lines of girls in blue streaming
out of doors when the fire bell thunders; the steady
drizzle of calculus and British novels; the words
that bead upon blank paper. In French
it rains step-siblings and great grandparents:
une demi-soeur, un demi-frere, une arriere
grandmere, un arrier grandpere.
In biology I study why I learn nothing;
the cerebral cortex is sheathed in a yellow
slicker; it has molded the medulla into a bucket
and bails facts out my ears. Which slosh
into the phone. "Creative writing classes
like it when you say stuff like rain is a
potato." So I'm telling you what I feel
and what I eat: that rain is a root
growing underground; that rain smells old
and dusty like a potato; that rain is crunchy
when raw, that rain is in me and on me
like a potato in a pot. That tonight,
under a streetlight, I saw rain hit pavement
and sprout white eyes.

Sarah Nooter

Aeneas Leaving His Dido

Inside his head
these words melted
then thickened like

butter: "build worlds
on worlds on
worlds."

They coated
his thoughts
and every desire

even his desire
for her skin
which was cool

and quiet as milk
and flowed around
his touch like

mud. Every hole in him
became like a
trumpet, blasting

these commands.
Even his ears
spread in glory

and shined
finally able to
deafen.

They screamed.
They told her
that he was

leaving
to build worlds.
She became

old, suddenly.
Her nails grew,
her touch was

a splinter to
him. Her eyes
seemed to

lose their
whites. Her eyes
grew   smaller.

He knew that
she wanted him
inside her

little eyes.
But what she
really wanted

was his thumb
in her tummy.
She told him

in a voice that
had soothed all
Africa of a tiny

boy, who had
stuck his thumb
into a pie

and come out
with a plum.
She wanted the

plum. She whispered
of her pie-like
features—

her depth, her
full taste. She
wanted wanted

that plum. She always
had needed a plum
inside her.

She always had wanted
milk climbing
her veins.

When he left for
his projects
she nursed

her poor body
which was small
in every way

and, really, had
never been like
pie to any man.

Sara A. Newland

Seven Veils

1.

most accounts agree

John's voice cooled their fetid souls
so she killed him

whether Herod ordered her killed
is open to debate

seven was the number of layers
until her sex
became
dangerous

2.

what if she had left the last one on?

3.

her mother: Salome, dance for me
Herod: Salome, dance for me
it's all so Freudian

4.

killing god's voice
is always
a bad
idea

5.

moon, wine, silver platter,
swords, shields, blood,
hair, lips, skin, everything
glistens

6.

didn't anyone teach you
violence against women begins at home
?

7.

seven was the number of sins
divided between mother and father-in-law

they weren't
the ones
who died

Note: "Seven Veils" is based on Oscar Wilde's retelling of the Biblical story of Salome. Salome's mother, Herodias, is involved in an illicit relationship with her dead husband's brother, King Herod. Herod lusts after Salome, who in turn is obsessed with John the Baptist, who is imprisoned in Herod's court. Angered by John the Baptist's condemnation of her mother's sinful relationship with Herod and fascinated by his prediction of the coming of a new Kingdom of God, Salome tries to win his affection, but is harshly rebuffed. When Herod offers to give Salome anything she desires if she will dance for him, she does so, shedding seven veils as she dances, and requests the head of John the Baptist as her reward. Herod reluctantly grants Salome's request and, after watching her lavish attention on the severed head, orders her killed.

Annie Lee

Regal Concubine[1]

They say I am the Delilah[2] of the T'ang dynasty.[3]

[1] Yang Gway Fay: one of most beautiful in Chinese history & most evil of wenches, making Emperor T'ang Ming Hwa stray away from duties to think only

[2] of RC and sex. Naturally, empire was crumbling and government officials started to plot RC's death, some treason and seizure of the empire. So it came to pass that during a revolt, Emperor TMH and RC fled palace (with servants and trusted government officials, of course) and came to hide in a monastery. The enemy was catching up. The story

[3] has three endings. Version one: as Emperor TMH, et al. are fleeing, RC commits suicide because she realizes she is root of all evil, with her beauty and seductive ways, and only her death can allow emperor to be good king again and save the dynasty. Version two: as Emperor TMH et al. are fleeing, government officials murder RC (for the sake of the nation, of course). Version three: as Emperor TMH et al. are fleeing, government officials attempt to murder RC but she is saved by a soft-hearted monk and brought to Japan where she lives out the rest of her days.

Rebecca Schonberg

4.5.199-235 [Exeunt Ophelia and Gertrude]

She would've regretted the step she took the second
after she took it.

A little older than me, hair longer,
eyes greener: she would've watched her dress flare out around her
letting the thirsty fabric drink
kicking her legs hard under the cloud of her clothes
breathing in,
and out,
river.

She would've regretted the step she took the second
after she took it.

She would've closed her eyes tight
squeezed
closed
out
of them until her eyelids melted
and then one foot and then the other, her ankles
shins waist chin eyes
over the edge, she would've gagged, again and again,
heaving up sludge,
and sucking down water, her eyes
greener still
with fern-light and loss.

She would've combed stars from her hair
with her liquid lines of fingers
and shimmered as she sank
that mysterious line threading beneath her face—
sane, not sane, sane, not sane, alive,
not alive,
exhaling waves of green glitter,
drifting irresistibly downwards through the shine.

She would've given "crazy" a new name
spoken softly and with lowered eyes,
and all the fishes nestled in her final breaths,

beckoning to her like the spent fingers of dead men,
would've known only
to swim around her, like angels,
around and around
trying to save
their crazy fish souls, all but lost
in the ripples she shed.

Renada Rutmanis

Queen of Hearts

Not all Kings have crowns
with which to slit their throats.
She raises her glass in sudden fury
and, no longer armed with husbands,
she says a silent prayer
to the keeping of secrets.

Rebecca Givens

Letter from the Artist

There it is: a square
falling into a square. Cubic,
three-dimensional place.
It's what your rocks are
made of, your graveyards,
dimly lit lands. It's what
you've learned to notice
around you, what you've
tried to project into flat space.

Put your hand up to it:
the canvas is a plane. No
one gives it the authority
of depth. It's your eye
that reaches back, watches
for the vanishing point.
It's you who see yourself
a field peasant, who paint
yourself a mirror of the page.

Rebecca Givens

Picasso's Painting

There is a total of three things
I wish to discover here. My life
is only so long. I want to know
how much can be said with the
white page and the thin line of
my pen. I want to know how
I look, drawing with my eyes
closed. Finally, I seek to learn
what motions it takes to make
a dove spring from the eye of
a woman, what measure of love.

Eric Wubbels

Picasso Was a Fly

Picasso was a fly
a darting, bloated horsefly
hovering over the scalp of the world

when he bit,
he left welts
as the pearls that lay beneath art's skin
bubbled up to the epidermis,
struggling to burst forth

he saw the world with eyes of shattered glass
but he saw it all,
and all at once,
in a grotesque pile-up of facets,
wedges, and fractals

yet despite his splintered vision
his life's work was a mirror,
unblemished and lucid, into which
the world was forced to gaze

and see the horror of itself
(subsequently attributed
to the art). they shattered
the mirror, they swatted the fly,
but the welts remained and remain

Kurt Wubbels

The Voice of Robert Desnos

So much like the flower and the current of air
like the waterway like the shadows passing
like the smile glimpsed this historic evening at midnight
so much like everything happy and sad
its last midnight lifting its naked torso above belfries and poplars
I'm calling those lost in the countryside
the old corpses the young fallen oaks
the shreds of fabric rotting on the ground and laundry drying in the
farmyards
I'm calling tornadoes and hurricanes
tempests typhoons and cyclones
riptides
earthquakes
I'm calling the smoke of volcanoes and cigarettes
the smoke rings of luxurious cigars
I'm calling the loved and the lovers
I'm calling the living and the dead
I'm calling the gravediggers I'm calling the assassins
I'm calling the executioners I'm calling the pilots the masons the
architects
the assassins

I'm calling the flesh
I'm calling she I love
I'm calling she I love
I'm calling she I love
triumphant midnight unfolds its satin wings and lands on my bed
belfries and poplars bend to my desire
those there collapse those there fall back
those lost in the countryside are found in finding me
the old cadavers rejuvenate at my voice
the young fallen oaks wrap themselves in greenery
the shreds of fabric rotting in the earth and on the earth flap taut at
my voice like the standard of
revolt
the linen drying in the farmyards dresses adorable women that I
don't adore

who come to me
obey my voice and adore me
tornadoes turn in my mouth
hurricanes redden, if it is possible, my lips
tempests snarl at my feet
typhoons, if it is possible, dishevel my hair
I receive the kisses of the drunkenness of cyclones
riptides come to die at my feet
earthquakes don't shake me but make everything totter at my order
the smoke of volcanoes dresses me in its vapors
and that of cigarettes perfumes me
and the smoke rings of cigars crown me
the loves and love so long pursued take refuge in me
the lovers listen to my voice
the living and the dead submit and greet me
the first coldly and the second familiarly
the gravediggers abandon their partly dug graves and declare that I
alone command
their nocturnal labors
the assassins greet me
the executioners invoke the revolution
invoke my voice
invoke my name
the pilots navigate by my eyes
the masons get vertigo on hearing me
the architects leave for the desert
the assassins bless me
the flesh pulses at my call

she I love does not listen to me
she I love does not hear me
she I love does not answer me.

Kurt Wubbels

(French) Public Transit

You carried your hair like a blanket
draping the walls and bedsheets you passed with its scent.

All along the hundred miles of quicksilver
French and English alike call Eurostar
you looked out from your window seat,
reading the countryside
for lack of a better book.

Paris brought the steel dragon of the Eiffel Tower
crawling from the bowels of the Centre Georges Pompidou
and the wine to forget the nightmare of the French themselves
as I slept in bewilderment in your arms.

Standing conspicuously closer
riding the same boxcars you said
Himmler ran in and out of this very village
some fifty years before us.
the Métro flung musicians, philosophers and lovers
through the spokes of the Apollinist city
and I clung to the pole with you to my chest
smiling at myself in the glass of the doors—

Narcissus asking his reflection why he is beautiful.

Jean-Paul Sartre, "l'Oracle Parisien"
responded the flower's beauty simply was.
To ask why is to ask for permission to be here
under this city, on the 12th of April,
of the moths who flutter around the absurd little incandescent
light-giving pears that dangled from the boxcar roof.

Joey Roth

Mishima on a Plate

I found a small version
Of Yukio Mishima,
On a plate.

He ordered a glass of orange juice
But when he tried to drink
He fell in.

His tiny body was mummified
By the citric acid
Which was a kinder death than his suicide.

He was alive for just a moment while in the glass
And he said something vague
About Japanese nationalism.

IV
In My Grandmother's House

Ben Lerner

In My Grandmother's House

In my grandmother's house
the shadows have begun to steal.

Slyly at first
they snatched a few dollars from the coffee table.

But now they have begun to grow bold
taking her memories in handfuls.

Soon she will be left with nothing
but the thin jacket she brought with her from Phoenix.

Marianna Green

Nowhere

A few minutes after she died, Dad sat staring at the corner of the hospital room because he once read in the *Time* "Afterlife" series that spirits are supposed to hover there. He said that my mother and I should also face the corners, say goodbye and tell her how much we loved her; as if we had not been saying goodbye all night; as if she did not already know.

I opened the window facing a typical Fresno highway littered with produce from overflowing tomato trucks, the four lanes separated by a median of dusty fig trees. Fresno. The name means ashes in Spanish and because of that fateful dubbing it seemed as though the lives of its residents were sheathed in a thin film of gray.

The road oozed a phosphorescent rainbow that always follows the first rain of winter. When Mom had called the night before she told me to drive fast, but not too fast. The roads were slippery, she said, and she did not want to lose me as well...that her losing her mother was bad enough, and her voice sighed in a drawn-out reaching for comfort, undercut by the morbid desire to beat herself up over the inevitable.

I packed a black sweater dress, several slices of processed chicken cold cuts in a plastic baggie, and a strand of pearls, tailgating the harvest moon through Salinas, Gilroy, and the San Joaquin valley. Mom was right—the pavement felt slimy under the wheels and the gearshift felt slimy under my palm. I stopped at a trucker joint halfway there to use the phone and studied a Mexican taking a piss from the flatbed of his low rider, as Mom informed me that a coma had just settled in. "Enough is enough," Grandma had growled in her thick Jersey accent. "I'm going to bed. Wake me up at seven 'cause I have needlepoint at eight," and with a last tug at the oxygen tubes that slithered down her nose and throat, she slept.

I knew that Dad was facing the corner because he could not stand to look at Grandma's corpse, could not stand to look at her forearms where the blue of her veins was indistinguishable from the graying skin, could not stand to look at her breast in anticipation of an impossible rise and fall. Mom, however, dabbed Grandma's silent pulse points with lady perfume and brushed back the hair from her forehead with a soft, bristled brush, revealing a silver-crested widow's peak. Mom also tried to close Grandma's mouth, which lay open and slack, but so heavy was her lower jaw that the usually pearly, powdered cheeks stretched down deep into her fallen chest, as shiny and as stiff as molded rubber.

When I had entered St. Agnes' Hospital the previous night, a flock of pinch-faced nuns pointed me the way to Grandma's room with dry, bitten, extended fingers, reminding me to slow down my gait. "Young lady, for the love of God don't run in the halls," they chanted. "The patients need quiet so that they can commune with our Father," droned one particularly fat nun from behind a computer screen. So I ran, and to me it seemed as if I ran as fast as I had driven, only now I sped by mountains of insulin, towers of bed pans, and fields of the old, the dying and the dead. I knocked my feet hard against the antiseptic floors in an effort to force life back into a place where there was none or soon would be. And I came to the room I somehow knew to be hers. The door was closed, the lights off, and through a slit in the diaphanous curtains I perceived the figure of my mother with a bottle of Windex, repeatedly scrubbing the mirror in which she stared at the reflection of her own mother behind her, as the feeble, erratic waves from the heart monitor streamed on. On the door was a small chalkboard that read:

Room 17
Name: Anna Nina Paladino
Age: 78
Condition: (blank)
Cause: Emphysema
Marital Status: Widowed
Insurance: Medicare
Allergies: dairy products & hair spray

I licked the sweat off of my upper lip, and with a flat palm pushed all the hair back from my face. The chalkboard stared at me, black with white, and the nuns in turn stared at me, in their black with white. I clasped the stainless steel doorknob with both wet palms, and pressed my right hip against the door to help it open.

After Dad was finished with the corner he moved to open the window, murmuring that the Indians believed a spirit needed an opening to escape from so that it would no longer be attached to a world in which it did not belong. A few nights before, Dad had watched a PBS special on the Native Americans of North America. He sat, blank-faced, the blue of the television illuminating the front part of his body, as a re-enactment of a funeral pyre scene flashed into his consciousness. The shaman of a Northwest tribe anointed a stack of redwood logs with lavender oil and scattered fragrant pine needles over the body. Then the gathered tribe swayed, humming and chanting as the wood, lavender, pine, and flesh rose in ashen curls and curves of smoke. One woman stood stony-eyed, her head raised towards the heavens, as a light layer of ash settled on her face, dulling the blue-black of her lashes and brows.

I headed towards the door as Mom was removing the get-well-soon cards from the bedside table and plucking out the wilted flowers from a sympathy bouquet.

"Where are you going, love?" she asked, her back to me, hands deep in a basket of yellow and pink flowers.

"Can I go for a walk?" She turned my way, one hand full of limp daisies, the other holding a petalless rose. "I mean, do you want me to stay here? This is...it is...." I pointed to Grandma. I always thought that people were rushed off after they died in a hospital, rushed off into another room where a futile attempt at resurrection was made, after which a doctor would return to the waiting family, head bent and shiny from perspiration, and everyone would know what he meant when he said, in a soft, throaty voice, "I'm sorry."

But she had been there exactly the same since she died, half an hour before. The doctor had pronounced her dead, switching off the flatlining heart monitor and cutting the flow of oxygen. There had been no "I'm sorry's," just a nod when he entered and a nod when he left. Periodically, a nun would peer into the doorway, asking us if we needed a priest or a drink of water. When the three of us shook our heads at both offers, she would shuffle away with a shrug of her bony shoulders, and I would resume looking at Mom, looking at Dad, looking at Grandma, and looking away, ears attuned to any sound at the door from someone who could tell me what to do.

Mom began, studying her own words as she spoke them. "Love, you seem to...." She dropped the flowers into the wastepaper basket. "You seem to have a tendency to flight."

"Huh?"

She walked over to me and holding my face close to hers tucked some wisps of hair behind my ears. And after a long, deliberate calculation, Mom said, "It is not noble."

"Wait...what?" I pushed her hand away and frowned at her in question.

"I don't know where you got it from. Certainly not from me." She moved away and sat on the edge of the hospital bed, her warm hand over Grandma's cold one, "And certainly not from your father."

I looked over to the window, where I imagined Dad to be precariously seated on the sill, but instead his body was halfway out, his head and torso soaking up the drizzle, while he hummed in a voice foreign to me, foreign to him.

"Do you want something? From downstairs. I mean, can I bring you back anything?"

"Anything?" She glanced around the room, her eyes resting for a second on each corner. "No. No, love, I don't think you can." So I left her, sitting on the foot of the bed, and headed downstairs to the cafeteria.

There, I bought a carton of grapefruit juice from concentrate and stirred in two packets of sugar. Then from my purse I took out the chicken, tore each piece into long slimy strips, watching as the cream flesh turned subtle shades of okra and orange under the singing fluorescence. A few minutes later in the parking lot I lit up a cigarette. My eyes traced the hospital building, searching for the figure of my father in every window, waiting to see him slip out of anxiety, waiting to see Dad topple from his own perch of mourning.

This time on my return down the hall I walked slowly and silently. The nuns did not look up and I did not look over. Mom was talking to the fat one behind the computer, making the final arrangements and I spied Dad walking duck-footed in the direction of the bathroom. The lights were on in Room 17, and I noticed that her bed was empty and already remade. The chalkboard on the door was void as well, and sweeping its surface with my fingerfips, I looked down at my hands newly covered in a thin film of gray.

The service was open casket. At first Mom insisted on having Grandma cremated, saying that six feet under the earth was no place for a lady to be. But Dad maintained that we would need a place to go and talk to her.

"The air is nowhere. You can't talk to the air."

So we decided on a cemetery located in between an artichoke field and an orange grove, and picked a plot shaded by an ancient fig tree. It was also situated next to a bell tower that sang out every hour and chimed a song at high noon. Mom said that Grandma would like the music.

It was still foggy the day of the funeral. I wore my black sweater dress, but left the pearls in my purse. The group of women from Grandma's needlepoint class all wore bright colors, saying that Grandma would not have wanted her funeral to be a morose occasion. They said that I looked like death, that I needed some rouge, and one asked if my grandmother's sense of style was absent in me.

But Mom wore a black dress as well, only no one commented on her lack of festiveness. At the gravesite, after everyone else had given their condolences and left, Mom leaned against the fig tree, looking at the coffin before it was to be lowered into the ground, looking at the mountain of flowers beside it. "I wish they had given those to her when she was alive. She always loved pretty flowers."

Dad stood by the coffin, petting it. Then he padded around to the far corners of the graveyard, hands behind his back, reading the inscriptions on the other headstones. I followed him to where he paused and sat cross-legged, his back propped up against an old monument in a particularly ancient section of the graveyard, his hands moving around, deep in the surrounding wet, overgrown grass.

"This is good," Dad looked up at me and nodded. "Yes, this is good. You see, the ground, it is everywhere."

Driving back home, somewhere in between Hollister and Gilroy, the rain died down to mist. I stopped at the same trucker joint as the one on my way to Fresno to call Mom and Dad, who were still there, going through all of Grandma's stuff, putting the house in mothballs.

Mom answered. "Your father went to Mexico for awhile," she whispered after a few seconds. "He said he needed to smell the ocean. He said that he needed to sleep on Mexican earth and see Mexican stars. I told him that there was plenty of land in California and that the whole world shares the same stars, but he said it was different. He said he needed to get away from all this gray weather. He said that she was the string that held this family together. He said he did not know. That he really didn't know."

"Oh, God," I said softly. "I'm sorry," again, my throat becoming tight and constricted, "I'm so sorry."

After that, the conversation died down to silence. Mom said to drive nice and slow on my way back home. She said that there was no rush, and we hung up as we always did, never saying "goodbye," just "see you soon."

I walked back to the car and, opening the door, stood looking at the fields of the San Joaquin Valley running up to the base of the mountains, looking at the mountains as they shrugged their shoulders high in the sky. The sky—only different consistencies of air, only variations of wet and dry, light and dark, dust and clarity. Air in shades of black, growing to peach, waxing to blue and waning to gray. Looking out, looking over, and looking up I saw the air and that the nowhere quality of it was everywhere. Face tilted back, open to the mist and the wind, my eyes drained quietly down my jawline and neck, and I realized that the ground is what is nowhere, that there was no steady ground. No ground to stand on at all.

Phoebe Prioleau

In My Uncle's Kitchen

You wipe your hands on the apron,
lean back against the door.
I say: "Tell me more.
Tell me more, I can handle it."
You scrape diced onions into a pan.
They spit and hiss. The noise calms us down.
You pull out a paper peel
from the pan. I prepare to listen. You say:
"I just can't deal
with the kids gone, Hepatitis C. I'm in
a downward spiral. It will take so much time
to heal."

You tilt the onions to the side,
turn down the flame.
"Trying to hide
tattoos is a waste of time. It never goes,
you know—the dirt, the grime
of back then.
I just think back on when
the kids were young. Ella broke her glasses
on the jungle gym at school. I made so many
big mistakes. I tried to act cool
when I shouldn't have—"
You pause, wipe your eyes, say,
"It's the onions, onions always make me cry."
In the pan I see the onions burn,
see the black creep along the edges,
but say nothing. It's not my turn
to talk.

Phoebe Prioleau

Mother's Ritual

You wear an old black flannel blouse
for the occasion. Worn. Stained from
past weeks, past years. Aluminum
alligator clips between your teeth,
sleeves rolled up to elbows.
You touch washcloth to bottle, washcloth to hair.

Dabbing your roots, you pause.
Your natural color
I've never seen. Brown. Auburn, perhaps.
Deep red like Granny's. "Grey doesn't suit me,"
you say, tossing the empty bottle into the
bathroom waste basket.
"I'm a 'Cherry Essence' kind of woman."

The black and white photos in your
honeymoon scrapbook are out of focus,
hide the truth. Hippie braids and
straw hats cover things up.
I want to know now
whether you looked like me.

Amy Kenna

The Duel

Roughly three-quarters crazy,
you face me.
Using the broom—
that blue-handled kitchen friend—
as a thing of threat, how *absurd*
and yet how petrifying.
The veins in your neck bulge—
tributaries feeding
to your mouth, swollen with
spring rage.
Ha!
Swing, swing again,
that sweet fan of straw on a stick,
your stabbing saber.

In one gradual moment
we become aware
of an understanding which surpasses
oral explanation. Our bellowing
is mutually unintelligible,
like two dialects of silence.
Reciprocal respect gleams
in both sets of eyes as
you raise the broom,

but then something shatters—
the dining room chandelier.
Broken glass rains down in
opalescent streaks;
we are both dismayed,
and everything
is in pieces again.

Katie Nichol

Regard to My Parents' Weakness

And I remember
my father
pulling to the side of the road
screaming at my sister
fuck you
Jessie, our neighbor,
sat still
too scared to unbuckle and run
goddamn it, just shut the fuck up
again
leaving echoes in me
like church bells on Wilson Avenue

The same spot in our house
that he first slapped me
I saw my mother cry
standing naked over the laundry,
mascara marking rivers
on her cheeks

My mother's tears fall eagerly
against the lot of our tempers,
as years accumulate and
dams break down
The water just flows

I have inherited
his quietness that builds up
the way an empty burner turned on
seems so unthreatening,
goes unnoticed
but given the chance
can melt plastic; skin
High temperatures
will burn food and flesh
and heat cleanses,
purifies what remains neutral or delicate
in our lives

Julia Schaffer

Nine Months Before September 4, 1977

This had nothing to do with me.
It was a tickle inside the elbow and toothpaste
on the breath that led to something
small and common,
a blue clasp of trust.
They warmed themselves in December, shutting out
light from cab horns and the 24-hour drug store.
It was a coincidence that I found form
like a ghost to murmur
above their moment
since no one was thinking about me
but my sister who lay awake with the smoke of dreams
sticking on her cold tongue
choking the impulse to run into their room and
furrow between them.
They slept soon, sinking into the mattress like honey.
My sister lay awake,
her bones were marbles on the mattress.
An insomniac at five,
she lay alert with a vision of a
heartbeat wrapped in tissue paper.

Samara Adsit Holtz

What Protects

That time we waited for her
by the black screen door.

We could see her shadow
in the porch light long before she saw
us, its long angles
suggesting a deep glamour that we
craved. As if the woman coming home
to us might have forgotten
duty and certainty.

She would know only
a random restlessness and beauty;
her hair splayed across her shoulders,
her dress pervious, twilit silk.

Instead, we recognized the steps
outside as those of our lilting
reconciliation.
As the door opened, we pulled further into
the corners of the darkened front room,
waiting for her hands
to find ours, with the touch
of someone who knew that we looked
for her rescue
and would never escape.

Talia Neffson

To My Father

Today I saw the storm sweep in
and watched at the window with you as the sky turned green.
I noticed a family having coffee in their garden,
no one reading newspapers;
they barely noticed the weather until a handful of droplets
        clung to their eyebrows.
We could have warned them if we were lower down.

We smelled the rain, or I think we did,
a minute or two before the sky performed its symphony.
Wow, you said,
amazing.
And I remembered how purple and recordable the sky
        had seemed last night.
Only appropriate I thought—
as my mother walked through the door, banging it to
        the first note of thunder—
that I will remember this forever.

Rina Nilooban

Sage

tea leaves crushed gingerly
on the jellied toast
sit on the sill and
catch incoming flights of wind
they rest gently on the crusts
as the smoke curls fell to the
tip of the gunboat carrying my mother and me
from the islands when the men
with tartar-green shirts came at night
to take the clock in the living room
and the porcelain vase with our pride inside
we fled to feel safe with the bass
squeezed for just enough comfort
against the ice packed closely on our spines
still the scent of the tea
mingling with the rosemary
mother had used to create her last work of art
remained in my mind and in my throat
and i whispered to her about
my visions of old spinsters under the balite*
and the banana trees sagging with their load
of thousands of moons clinging to their branches
and asked if i would ever touch
them again

so she took the tea leaves
cupping them as a tot would
balance a fresh wobbling chick
and she raised her palms to
touch my quivering nose and the
currents of the tea swirling inside
as passionate and colorful as incense
carried me in their crests
over mangos in bunches in carts on the streets
among the rice paddies and
if i let myself slip
i might waddle in the water again
and feel free with

everything and nothing rushing around me
and the expanse of the checkerboard land
engulfing me
as the sea of the womb
did in the beginning and
it cradled me
i found my home in
a bed of mango peels

The balite is a type of tree indigenous to the Philippines.

Rina Nilooban

Why I Didn't Visit the Doctor's Office

i never completely understood
how when i was seven and
playing tea with imaginary pals,
my father, the pediatrician, would
rave and scream about mess
and other odds and ends that
were a "sore in the eye"
and i would squint at the white area
that was now red-rimmed and
feel guilty for giving my father a booboo.

i always wondered why the girls and boys
whom he paternally stuck Band-Aids on
and gave heaps of "My Doctor Loves Me" stickers to
also got all the smiles
and the much-needed-at-seven
psychological talk that relieves
the inward pains of a knee scrape
and how i always managed
to catch scorching glares
and smacks on the behind for reading
when i should have cleaned the toaster.

i would juggle explanations about my father
and why i didn't get the stickers
why my screams were more irritating
than the neighbors' brats
and how he said he loved me
by being a provider
i could only guess that my father, the pediatrician,
gave so generously of his lollipops
that when it was my turn
he had reached the bottom of the bag.

Rebecca Ciralsky

Monsoon

"What do you think about sex
in high school?" my mother asks
randomly as we are driving,
her hands clutching
the wheel matter-of-factly
as if she were discussing clothes
or maybe a trip to Mexico to visit
David. *"What do I think?"* is all
I can manage to blurt out, my mind
rewinding to that night
in the car with the droplets of rain
plunking on the roof, his hand
fumbling with the pearlized buttons
on the black silk V-neck shirt I bought
at the Gap and had worn that time I
went in to get extra help in math and
later realized that the top button had
come loose revealing the tops of my
breasts. *"What do I think?"* stuttering
now, hardly believing that I am
having this conversation as we pull out
of First Star Bank and head
down Brown Deer Road to Kohl's
Department Store. This is definitely
worse than the assembly at school
where those dancers came on stage
moving to country music with lyrics
about wearing a condom. I had buried
my head into the shoulder of the guy
next to me, embarrassed for the dancers.
I turn my face to stare at the cars along-
side us as she says, *"Well I hope that*
when you get to that stage, you will
talk to Dad and I and use birth control."
Why had I stayed
in the room last night watching
the *20/20* special report on teenage
sex by Barbara Walters, ensconced
between mother and father, no one
saying a word not even
during commercials when Dad used to give
me the tickle torture, all of us edging

around the subject with silence, like
those books that they had bought for
me with titles like *Where Did I Come
From* and *What is Happening
to Me,* with the pictures of pink naked
girls and boys, sperm with smiles, and
different shaped breasts, these books
that were supposed to hold
all the answers, but that I found hidden
within my dad's colored sock drawer.

Rachel Schwartz

In the Basement

Under the kitchen floor
and pipes,
everything is amplified,
metallicized.

Between turbulent breaks of silence,
Mom standing right side, Dad left,
it's like a mess hall,
a massacre—
thrown place settings and smashed counters,
"fuck's" and "she's."
"She hurts me more than you."

I thought about our old house
and how we used to grow sunflowers in our back yard:
Only three,
rising up against our green metal fence.
Annual or perennial?
I couldn't remember.
But they were tree-sized,
at least two feet taller than me at age eight.
I wanted to pick the seeds out of the flower heads.
But when I looked up,
I couldn't see anything—
the sun and all.
I couldn't see.

"She hurts me."
A break of silence.
Then Dad crosses to the right of the room
and leaves.

We never planted any here.
And I thought just for a moment
that maybe I could plant a field of them
right upstairs in the kitchen.
The sky-sized ones.
Enough flowers to keep them separated,
keep them from walking over the pipes
and smashing the counters.
From the "She hurts me more's."

Just enough so they can't see.

Jaime Halla

Rental

A white Dodge Infinity,
smeared with old snow
and salt, just for today.
The wind hisses through
creases between doors
and windows. Stale, crackled
menthols cut into new leather.

Eating western omelets
and greasy silence, planning
responses to backhanded
questions. Antiques
and my mother's love
life are not my idea
of enthralling conversation,

but I answer. I lie.
I suddenly can't recall
what happened to the
drafting desk, or what
my mother did last
Saturday night, while he
was shooting pool alone.

So every few months
I sit on rented leather
and listen to crackling
menthols, hoping he
won't ask to come
inside of the house
that used to be his.

Christopher Lew

Country

On Sunday mornings, Dad
puts on country music
in the kitchen. Country,
where men and women sing
about love, new love in sticky
summer heat, and old love,
the kind with a fat wife.
With the radio on low,
Dad leans against the washing machine
and remembers the honeymoon in Montauk.
Dad called Mom *Meatball*
and watched the afternoon
charter boats pull in at five
as Mom sat cross-legged on the bed
studying for her bachelor's
from Brooklyn College.

Now Mom's administration.
She's at school hiring
a new teacher, and writing up
a bad one that's balding.
Dad never has dinner ready
when Mom toots the horn
and pulls in the driveway.
Each night is an experiment:
extra cornstarch,
a couple of basil leaves,
that packet of MSG from the Ramen
noodles. After dinner, Mom runs
to the computer to finish up work.

In the kitchen, Dad turns the radio on.
There's too much to do:
the clothes sit wrinkled in the dryer,
the stink rises from the water main,
the phone rings—the dry cleaners
can't take the spot out
of the brown dress. He washes

dishes stacked in size order,
soaps the chopsticks, warped
and bent like bad spines.
The sponge slides over a fistful,
as if wanting to straighten them
all at once. He rinses
a pair off, puts them next
to the forks and soup spoons,
rests his arms against the sink,
and listens to that song about
old love.

Ian Demsky

North Wind Testament

The dusty spoor of a comet unwads
in a hurtling sneeze
across the face of this cold,
or that cragged, rock with blue scrapes

like where along the complexion
of our dead uncle's pickup truck two parallel smiles
were carved by a night of debauched gestures.
Even Aunt Maxine
(who still uses the last name Nunes
of her first husband, a loud Portuguese)
knew where he was that night: A blonde girl
from the local community college
cheeks red from showering
and a few neat glasses of whisky.
The wedding band
in the back pocket of his jeans under
his wallet on her floor on top of her

fuzzy blue sweater. Tonight the weather report
boasted two inches of snow in
Maine and we know that winter here
in southeastern Michigan isn't far off.
Aunt Max puts the children to bed and we watch
the pencil-thin trestle of light sweep
across the sky and she decides maybe
it's best she never gave birth to a boy.

Karen Emmerich

Phone Booth, 10 p.m.

Last night you called
from some strange city to say
you were sorry about all those
pills and the gasoline
and you promised to stay well
if only I would come visit
and not bring you back
to the hospital. Then you asked
what day it was, and did I know
where it was that you
were supposed to be?

Monday, I said, and no.

Caitlin Doyle

Aftermath

When I grow up
I want to specialize in Aftermath
I will appear at fires, crashes, explosions
to join the screaming survivors.
You'll know me as a panicked glimpse
behind the news reporter on your TV.
I'll make my body an accident antenna,
moving from disaster to fresh disaster,
Until my face in your living room
seems like furniture,
or family.

Mike Livshits

Is Burning

Tonight I sit on the kitchen
Table, the lightbulb's warm breath
On my neck. I am remembering times
When I should have cried.

The time I brought home Stella,
Who had a face like a horse and braids
On the left side of her head, she'd
Said, "What should I say to her, Tina?"
Then my mother opened the door
And stepped back without a glance
To let us in.

In the kitchen the night before, mother had said,
"you don't know what loving a man is like. It's sweet
and satisfying and"—
she shifted her gaze from
my right to my left ear—
"normal."
I wanted to be
The dyke she thought I was.
I said, "You don't know what eating
Cunt is like."
She picked up the phone,
And without dialing a number,
Cried into it,
Poured her divorced unmedicated
Menopausal grief into it.
She cried into the phone through
Closed eyes until short beeps
Replaced the dial tone. Then she
Hung up and turned her back on me.
She leaned against the refrigerator
And peered into the reading lamp in the living room.
I could see each hair on her arm
In the light of the lamp.
I stood in the middle of the kitchen, dry,
Watching her square her shoulders,

Adjust an earring.
I didn't know Stella's birthday.

Or the morning my father left
To open his deli without kissing
Mother goodbye, and she picked up
The phone, and for the next hour it was
      "Samuel
      Samuel   Mí corazon
      Justina
      My daughter"
As she leaned her forearm on
The countertop, wearing only
Cotton panties and a white T-shirt.

When a runner finishes a race
They show you her unofficial time
A few minutes before the official time,
Because they don't want to keep you waiting.

When I was shown the unofficial time
For my parents' marriage,
X years, Y months, Z days,
I watched Scooby Doo, dry,
My finger hooking a big one from my
Six-year-old nose.
Mother stopped speaking to the phone.
She began crying into it. She promised it
That she would die without it.

Last week someone poured
Buckets of orange paint
On her grave
And four other Guerro graves near it.
I never cry.
The light is burning the hair
On the back of my neck.

Sara A. Newland

Finding the Body

We found them under the furniture,
Caleb's half-digested pills. For six weeks
they plagued us like rodents, creeping out
as we washed the floor, hiding under
the dinner table, behind the sink.
Thinking maybe he'd swallowed one,
we praised his strength. We didn't see
the bones pressing upward through his fur,
his yellow tongue hanging from the side of his mouth.
I was seven, and thought death
was something I could conquer,
as small as the mice the cats spent all night killing
then placed at my sleeping feet.

Sara A. Newland

Dreaming Grandfather's Funeral

We thought she'd be the first to go,
but here she is, serving coffee
to the aunts, congratulating Uncle Charlie
on turning 102, resting
her purple, withered hand on the piano
as she passes by.

Then it turns weird.

Mom pulls a mouse from her pocket.
I say "don't do that, you'll kill Grandma"
but she's having fun, the mouse
is white and brown and full of love.
My mother stands in the middle
of the room that Grandfather loved,
a circle of old women turns around her
like a wheel, drinking coffee, eating lox.
The mouse in her hand is squeaking
but none of them faint.

Sara A. Newland

Renascence

She lay in a blue wool suit,
the grandmother I hardly knew,
raised as if peering over the edge of her casket,
pearls flattening the folds of skin
on her neck. My mother said,
this is the way they do it
out here, they like watching
the dead. I liked it too,
watching her watch us
through blue-lidded eyes.
I half expected her to rise
from the coffin like a bird
I once thought dead,
then watched fly
through my open window.

David Konieczkowski

Marvin

Marvin never talked about what had happened to him in Vietnam. He never talked, but he did yell too much. We were in his basement, him sitting by the motorcycle he kept down there. It sat next to an old hole in the cinderblock wall, which the family kept covered with a maroon rug. He would sit on the motorcycle and talk with me. Do you remember, Marvin, do you remember saying, "Jeff's a good kid. I yell at him too much. I really do. You know it's true"?

Do you remember how we'd bob for apples in that basement on Halloween, cold steel tub and water and plunging down for apples before they shot back up? Or trying to break open the piñata, jumping to catch the candy dripping out of it? Do you remember the woman at the steel mill where you worked who said you called her a bitch and spat on her foot? I remember you, furious about that. I remember you smiling and hugging your wife when you proved it couldn't have happened—you were at home when she said you did it. You went back to work after that, worked and welded that steel. You made my father a belt buckle, steel on the outside and a fifty-cent Kennedy piece smiling out from in the middle, held together by steel cable welded and wound around the outside. Do you remember that when I was at your house, I would sleep in Jeff's room, and we'd sneak downstairs early in the morning to play Sega? Do you remember how Jeff and I would ride our bikes down the hill of your road, then go down to the woods behind your house and climb around? He sometimes left your tools out in the woods where they rusted, after he took them to carve his name into trees. You showed him once how to scrape the rust off the tools so you wouldn't yell at him.

Do you remember us leaving our dog at your house as our families went to church? He was a big old German shepherd, King. You would fill his water bowl, which we brought with us—blue and round and plastic. Do you remember driving us to church, dropping Jeff and me off, giving us quarters for the collection? We went to Sunday School next door to the church, and played Hangman with the teacher. She'd pick words like "Euphrates River," a phrase which somehow I knew as soon as she drew in the blanks, but she wouldn't let me tell Jeff. Do you remember how we'd join you then in the church next door? We never went down front, Jeff and I, when the minister called for all the children to come talk with him—we looked at each other and smiled. We weren't children. We were ten.

Do you remember how we'd come back from church and find the neighbor's son—I don't remember his name now—and climb on his family's tool shed? We were caught one afternoon in the summer, and spent three hours repainting the shed to cover up our footprints. Do you remember that, Marvin? Do you remember, back in Vietnam, the Agent Orange they sprayed on you in the jungles? I imagine they were hot and misty, not like your Ohio summers. I know you never talked about that. It never seemed to bother you, though I think it had to. I guess that was why you yelled too much. Maybe it was even why you loved Jeff and his sisters and your wife Mary Jane so passionately. I imagine that they cried with you in the doctor's office when you found you had cancer. I imagine that even you cried, sometimes, in the hospital, winter-white sheets pulled around you, matching that old welder's skin as it lay dying, though I wasn't there. I know you remember that.

Erica Magrey

Dear Tony

dear Tony,
my conceptions of you
were warped, selfish by default

standing about seven feet from your casket
I felt mom's forehead on my back, her hands
gripping my waist

the football team
stood assembled on my left
some red-faced quarterback squeezed the hand
of your son
he was wearing those damned Italian loafers
that you bought for him last spring

I was mainly disturbed
that when I knelt in front of you
a stagnant emptiness had replaced your poignant cologne
that I once choked on
I choked anyway
instinctively, I guess

Ian Demsky

AIDS

Then all at once a wrinkle somewhere in blood.
                                  A fold.
It wasn't in me. When something went out it came in
smelling of low tide.
                                  Crease.

It came in and held like dye.

Haven't gotten around yet to saying *Mom & Dad,*
your grandchildren can't come from me.

X's blood came back from the laundry soiled,
Y sports a gravy stain on the necktie in his blood

Don't worry I've been held the way I wanted. I tried all the positions
that looked interesting. I never really wanted children anyway.

Full of army wisdom, my grandfather used to say things like
Blow it out your barracks-bag or
                              They say you
never see
the one that gets you.

As if he knew then
it all would come down to

caissons of hemoglobin
and a difference of deadlines:

four letters, the last of which is Sanguine
as the caissons go rolling along...

Lucy Cutolo

Jewels

My mother says my sister Jewels get everything from her father. The way she's not happy unless she has ten pairs of shoes and how she's always caring about what other people think and how she'll never walk with my mother in town because my mother never wears a bra and her beads never match her shirt.

"That's the way her father was," my mother tells me. She cups my face in her hands. "But you, you are my shining star. Your father was my sun."

My mother had Jewels when she was eighteen. She was living in the suburbs with my grandparents. Jewels' father was at Princeton. Everyone thought my mother would marry him, but she didn't. After Jewels was born she packed up everything and went to India, to search for herself. Her parents said that if she left, she could never come back. So I don't know my grandparents; they've never seen me.

My father was French. He had green eyes and blond hair, like me. He met my mother in India. My mother said the night I was conceived, they wished on a star and it fell to earth and that's how they chose my name. A year and a half after I was born my father died. Jewels was five. He died in a car accident on a mountain road. So my mother left and came here, to Saraset, and bought a trailer to raise us in. My mother loves the desert. She said if she had to do it again she would have named me Sand. I'm glad she didn't, though.

My mother used to tell me how wonderful my father had been, and that I was just like him. She told me that Jewels had to learn, that we had to teach her the right way, and to stop loving "things" so much.

When I was ten I read an article about a boy named Jeremy Rose. He was a beautiful, famous boy, my age, and he was different, just like me. His family was like mine, his trailer was just like ours. I hung his picture next to my father's on my half of the wall. He is my Destiny, we are two sides of a coin.

My sister laughs when she hears me say this. My mother gets angry, her mouth twists and her eyebrows come together. She thinks that movies are awful and that Jeremy is a cardboard copy of a person. But I know that he is just like me. Someday, he will come to this nothing town and take me away.

Jewels turns eighteen next week. I hope she leaves. She's been strutting around like a peacock talking about getting a job in the city, but I know she doesn't have any money. Maybe she can live in a sand castle.

My mother's throwing her a party tomorrow. She's been reminding Jewels to come home early all week. She says it's "important." She's giving away the surprise. All my mother's strange friends from the bookstore where she works are coming. They ordered a cake shaped like a jewel. I was surprised. My mother doesn't like parties.

Jewels is sitting at the table with my mother when I walk in. My mother is nodding at her, drinking tea, the orange kind. With the tea in her right hand, she reaches back and pulls at the neck of her shirt.

"Don't you think it's time to start wearing a bra?" Jewels asks.

My mother shakes her head no, and smiles. It's late and they are going to fight, so I go to my bedroom.

Jewels's bed is overlapping the dresser and her blanket is on my side of the room. I pick it up and walk over to Jeremy. I close my eyes and lean against the wall. "I'm waiting," I say. The people in my family think it's strange that I talk to the wall, but I know that if I keep his picture up and talk to him every night, he'll hear me and find his way to his Destiny.

Jewels comes in and laughs. She turns off the light while I'm still standing so that I have to finish undressing in the dark.

The next morning the sun comes through the holes in the shades and wakes me up. My mother is on the phone with Sandy about tonight. She is the one who's bringing the cake. Jewels comes in yawning. My mother hangs up and turns around.

"Tonight...important...." she says.

Jewels shakes her head and rolls her eyes, "Important..." she mimics.

My mother laughs. She turns around and around, singing Bob Dylan. Jewels stands up and leaves. My mother sits back down and stops singing. She's smiling.

"Jewels is getting better," she sighs. "...so much I wanted to teach you children, about values, objects, love. Jewels has her father in her, she can't appreciate what we have."

What we have is a trailer the size of a raisin box, a broken TV, a sink that gargles dirt into our water and a green toilet that never fully flushes. The Porta-Potty at Albert's garage is nicer than our bathroom. Please, I think, please let Jeremy come and find me. I'm sure he's just like my father, strong and cool, with all the right values. I hope that we can keep our values and still get a house with clean water and a working TV.

Sandy comes over with the cake. It's beautiful, with chocolate ice cream and blue frosting. My mother says she hopes the freezer holds out until Jewels gets home.

Melinda and Eleanor arrive next. Jewels says they're lovers. They look alike, though, so I thought they might be sisters, but last month I saw them kissing outside of Lou Lou's Diner. I guess that that means they're not sisters. I love their hair, long and black, with blue in it. Jewels says they get the color from a bottle.

Everyone puts up streamers and Sandy goes to the store to buy candles. My mother stops and pulls me aside to show me Jewels' gift. It's a bright gold locket with a diamond in the center. It was from my mother's father to her. Inscribed, it says, *to my little girl, my precious jewel, love Popi.*

"I named her after the locket." She pauses and then swallows.

"My father used to call me Jewels." She laughs, "Dan, her father, wanted to name her Mildred after his grandmother." She puts the locket back in the box.

At seven-thirty, John shows up. I think my mother should date him; he has beautiful blue eyes. Jewels says she can't because he likes men. My mother's friends are confused. Jewels says they're queer, and leave it up to my mother to find the only queer people in the county of Saraset, but I don't think she should talk. Her boyfriend drinks, throws up and starts drinking again, and last weekend he threw up down his shirt and slept in it.

So here we are: me, my mother, Sandy, Eleanor, Melinda and John. The trailer is too small for all of us, so I go to my bedroom to wait. At eight o'clock, back in the too-small kitchen, my mother's neck tightens. Her cheek begins to twitch. She smiles at me and blinks.

At eight-thirty she sits on the kitchen stool and spins. Her skirt twirls up and snaps as she twists. John looks at Sandy, who checks the cake. I know it has begun to melt, because I checked ten minutes ago when everyone was looking out the window.

At nine o'clock Eleanor looks up from behind her hair. "We have to go," she says. "Remember? We could only stay an hour." Melinda puts her hand on my mother's shoulder, "We could stay," she says. All I can think is that they are lovers.

"No," my mother says. "Go."

At ten o'clock, Sandy leaves and the ice cream begins to drip out of the freezer. John clears his throat. I don't care that he loves men, right now he loves my mother. John begins to say something.

"Just leave," my mother snaps. Then she begins to cry.

"I love you, Carol." He kisses her on the cheek. My mother cries harder.

At eleven o'clock, the cake needs a bowl. Please. I close my eyes. Please, Jeremy. Come now. I see, in my head, the door open. I see his face, understanding the trailer, ignoring the river of ice cream. I know that he'll just hold me and love me.

My mother puts her hand on my shoulder.

"We thought we could change the world." She puts her head down. "I feel like all the things I passed on to you never touched Jewels." She turns around and shouts, "She's just like her lying bastard of a father."

All of a sudden Jewels is there, standing in the kitchen. "I hate you," she says. "At least my father wasn't a junkie, who hid from the world and died in a pit."

My mother slaps Jewels, hard. It's the first time I ever saw my mother hit anything. I doubt she would beat the rugs, if we had any. Jewels starts to cry.

"You're a liar," Jewels says. "All those years you lied to Star. You loved her more because she came from him, but you were just lying to yourself as well. I was five years old; I remember, you know." She turns to me as if she is really sorry and shrugs. "Carol lied to you," she says.

"He was beautiful." My mother turns around. "He was everything you and your father could never be. You get out." She starts to sob, her head bent low.

I watch in slow motion as they fight. The trailer is too small. It's as if we were all caged.

"Fine." Jewels walks into our room. Ten minutes later, she's gone.

My mother calls her friends and apologizes. She says the mix-up was due to the death of her oldest daughter. She doesn't even try to talk, to explain. She throws the locket away with the cake. The gold glitters from underneath the melted ice cream...*love popi*...thrown away forever.

I go into my room. It's just mine now. It looks empty without Jewels' shoes. I keep waiting for the light to turn off while I'm still standing, but it doesn't.

I take my father's picture down. I am not too disappointed. After all, all he was, really was, was an illusion, a dream of a person. I look into Jeremy's eyes. "I'm waiting," I say. I lie down on my bed with my eyes closed, waiting for my Destiny to come and find me, hoping he doesn't need a map, 'cause we're not on one.

Alexis Goldberg

The Shalimar Diner

I
i used to think it was the most luxurious place in the world
there are real lobsters swimming in the tank and the waitress
        would give me
two scoops with the dinner special, one vanilla and one chocolate.

the manager would recognize me every time i came in
and he would tell me how much i'd grown
and how much i looked like my grandmother
who was still, after all the years he'd known her, a very
        beautiful woman
(we needed no reassurance however,
we knew that we were from a long tradition of great beauty).

we'd always sit in the same section and the same
        bleached blonde waitress
knew what my grandfather was going to have even
        before he'd ordered.
nobody knows why, but my grandfather always asks for his
    Greek salad in a bowl instead of on a plate.

II
tonight is his seventy-ninth birthday and that is why we are here.
his Greek salad comes on a plate tonight.
this is not the same waitress i know, she has left like
        everything else familiar.

this may be the first night i have ever eaten in this diner without
    ordering the hamburger special
but in keeping with the lack of salad bowl
i order pasta, and suddenly i feel old.

without my grandmother here nothing is the same: the electric hand
        sensor in the bathroom is dingy instead
of exciting, the old women with the droopy faces waving their
        cigarettes in the smoking sections and
talking with Queens accents are not part of the allure anymore, and
        even the ms. packman game in the entryway is broken.

across the street the Ali Baba Catering Company still glistens, but
     you wouldn't know that if you hadn't seen it before because
     now the sign only reads: BABA CATERING INC.
the Ali, it appears, has left with my grandmother.

i am thinking about this as i eat vanilla ice cream sans the chocolate
     and as i walk to the bathroom and idly
run my hands under the sensor and as i walk to the ms. packman
     game and try my 50 cents.

it eats both quarters and won't give them back.

III
on the drive home i am thinking about lost innocence and my
          grandmother
and sorrow is not exciting, i have recently realized,
not an emotion, as i had previously thought it was,
all-consuming and melodramatic and tight,

but rather something that exists, that didn't before,
that nibbles at your edges
and that you can't fully comprehend the proportions of
except
at The Shalimar Diner.

V
Welcome

Susan Currie

Welcome

She watched the circus burn that day.
The tightrope fizzled
And fused itself to the safety net
Which collapsed around her feet.
The trapeze artists
Ran to shelter
Under the open sky becoming gray with smoke.
The elephants roared
As she came into adulthood flaming.

Nora Lawrence

Fourteen

Shouting back at the macho men
you can't have us, go home
skipping away under the street lamp
we could still feel them wanting us

I saw the misty rain in the air when I squinted
you sang as the cars whizzed by
smeared your cigarette butt
into the brick wall of the A&P
dropped it on the sidewalk

we exulted in our new independence,
showed off our teen age
to anyone who would look at us
I wasn't shy when I was with you—
talking to strangers
I startled myself with my arrogance

we sat on a wet stoop
and you told me stories
of the hearts you'd broken
I concentrated on reflections
of yellow headlights I saw
in the dark street
it was understood that you were lying
but the bullshit excited me anyway

Erin Walsh

Summer at Brooke's

In early June
we lay on the side porch
on the trundle bed mattress,
buzzing like June bugs at window screens.
Shadows from the bug candle
flowed across the paneled walls
as we crept out the side door,
leaving a crack open for the cats.
Whispering,
we shuffled through gutters
in our pajamas
to Woodson Park
and shared a midnight snack
of Ruffles and jelly sandwiches.
Brushing crumbs from our shorts,
we sprinted to the swings,
legs pumping like pistons.
We flew,
our toes pointed like angels
at the moon.

Ian Kain Amato

Were There Children?

Before I was born were there children who gathered their tears
from wells placed deep inside their empty bodies by their parents'
        bruised hands?
Were there children who watched, for hours, the running of other
        students' feet
over dusty playgrounds without moving?
Were there children who could not look in their own eyes
        in the mirror,
and whose bodies shook as violently as the ocean's white froth?
The ocean hypnotizes scared children like those who
grasped for their mother's breasts after her milk dried.
Were there children who knew they came from the ground,
and would go back,
knowing this as not bad?
Were there children who stared with open eyes into the sun,
although their grandparents told them not to?
Were they not afraid when their sight became dark
because they knew, as light filled their skin,
the sun shined only for them?

I am that child, sitting in a dark room, on a small chair,
as passing cars move a window of light across white walls.

Ian Kain Amato

Morning Thoughts

1. At the Beach

I opened my eyes to grains of sand,
and drew designs remembered from the time before birth.

I woke with the shells, and threw rocks at the waves,
knowing the ocean would not take my light body—yet.

Because of the stars watching me I was unable to sleep.
Lying on the ground I realized the earth has no eyes.
"I will be your eyes; you can see through me."

I scratched my red hands on the twilight dirt while digging.
Dirt gathered in my mouth as I went deeper, one grain of
          sand mixing in with all the others.

2. The Alone Child

I dreamed I was the moon in cold thought.
I glowed on the silver ocean, and in the night forest
I made visible the first fall leaf to escape its tree.

In an unknown house windowpanes magnified morning light
          on dark paintings
of splattered red and glowing eyes, inside rusty frames.
I waited with my morning thoughts.
My mother called me, "I made eggs!"
I am my mother's egg.

I stirred within the warmth of my mother
whose tangled blond hair covered a stranger's stomach.
Unable to remember whether my mom ever cuddled with me
I walked from her unconscious body until it was a distant speck.

3.

Awake with me on the ground.
I will be the rain covering your body,
breaking myself on your nipples,
then sliding over your hot skin into the earth.

I promise you will barely remember me.
I will be like a passing dream.

Alexis Goldberg

Momentary Mastication

In one fleeting moment
(before it pops)
I see my entire life
Reflected in a
Strawberry banana piece of
Bubblegum
And it scares me out of my mind

Nafeesah Allen

The Winter of My Life

The Heart of Spain vibrated through the brisk, pre-winter air and rasped lightly on my second floor bedroom window. I denied his offer, closed my manila curtains, and hoped that my actions would bid him my most cordial farewell. Finally, the tapping stopped. Assuming he had gotten the hint, I decided it was safe to open my curtains to invite the sunshine in for tea. But surprisingly, there he was, the Heart of Spain, perched on the black tar rooftop directly facing my bedroom window.

Day after day, he sat patiently, awaiting my inevitable arrival. Sometimes he slept on the patio de los vecinos, who live downstairs. Other times he played with el niñito, whom I often saw riding his bike in the six by eight foot cemented back yard, a back yard among a sea of back yards and rear terraces that have become the only face of España that I know. Nevertheless, the day he directly asked me if I knew how to tango, by simply singing some gentle Spanish words into my soul, was the precise day that I opened my window, stepped out onto my bright yellow, slightly soiled windowsill, tightrope-walked along my clothesline, and glided on air right into his arms. I danced the forbidden dance with the Heart of Spain. We rhythmically performed steps that included pirouettes from the balcony into the living room of some unsuspecting neighbor. Who would've ever thought that I and the Heart of Spain could somehow become one in this seemingly minuscule backdrop that has become my favorite landscape in all of Zaragoza, a landscape of azoteas, back yards, and balconies located directly outside the one window in my room?

We danced and talked all night long, and once he serenaded me under God's own purples and pinks and blues, the colors He uses to kiss the bright-eyed kids of all ages good night. And then the moon came out to play.

My eyes began to get heavy and after awhile his feet began to tire. We decided to move the forest of plants that some anonymous neighbor had arranged on the side of the rooftop facing my window. We slept under the stars, trapped in beauty. I woke up.

Alone.

"¡Mis Plantas! ¿Que has hecho?" screams my no longer anonymous neighbor.

"¡Ay Dios Mio!"

The brisk pre-season air returns and it is then I realize that my dream has ended. And a great reality is yet to come.

Now I have to find a way to get down from this godforsaken rooftop.

Nafeesah Allen

Virgin Rhapsody: Pearls

Silvery black metallic, slightly like Ethiopian silver, purple-black skin makes me sulk into the depths of my Americanism, and I turn my head away from these creatures. Colors that don't match and eyes that are not of hunger, but beg for me to look into them. Braided hair, screaming from the scalps of beyond nigga-nappy heads, grabs my attention and maybe if they spoke my language I would feel the connection that I am supposed to. Then again, maybe not. They sell scarves, ties and bootleg CDs from the bases of tired worn-out rags that have survived many a voyage and protect their products from the reality of the Zaragoza[1] streets. I despise them and, at the same time, I wish I could love them.

Light pink skies and blue sprinkles are strewn helplessly across the sky and bright clumps of white thrust themselves across the land-scape of my ancestors' home. This is where they once were. Kente clothes (real ones, not that industrialized print, made by small Korean children in underground factories, that is distributed to African-American bookstores across America) drawn from African herbs and fruits of the Earth, drape my great-great-great (a bunch more greats) grandmother's body as she gives birth to another ancestor who will later be torn from her arms, as she, herself, is thrown into the depths of a black past, hidden by the idea of civilization. She daydreams the image of how they have raped and beaten that child and she cries each night and wants to kill herself, for having brought life to some-thing so beautiful, in a world so cruel. This is the origin of my psyche.

And somehow, through an unidentifiable chain of events, I am here, sitting on a cold linoleum floor, listening to that music that "lulls lukewarm lullabies"[2] into a deaf ear, trying to express myself into an iMac, while my mind is scattered across the floor and the four walls surrounding me, in misspelled Spanish words. This is where fate has brought me, and this is me, spitting in his face.

African-American is the term by which they have chosen to define me. I am nothing and everything from Africa. I look into the faces of African people and I can admit, with something much more than a hunch, that I look down on them, with an ashamed state of mind that forbids me to look them in the eyes. They are underdevel-

172

oped, poor and worse off than I am. And they make me look bad. But as I identify myself on every college admissions application, I am African-American. I would love to feel something more than contempt, but it is not my fault. I'm not the first one to have been brainwashed, in white dyes and light colors of caramel, but never black. I remember that I'm seeing through eyes that are not my own.

If you ask me, my ancestry started in the American South, Deep South, in the depths of a land that bears nothing but sand and weeds from soil, filled with ant hills, drier than the Sahara. This is where I began. This is my birthplace. I was born in the rows of cotton fields in Alabama, where wooden slats served as walls in the fall and perspiration served as heaters in the winter.

I can still remember my great-grandmother's house, sitting on a road, fairly desolate, surrounded by that unfruitful soil. A small house, standing barely by the grace of God, with nothing to it but the smell of old people, and old plumbing and no air conditioning and long lost dust-balls. And as I look at old black and white pictures of deceased relatives, I receive the play-by-play of their poor sharecropper lives, from my great-grandmother. I smile and excuse myself as I go to the bathroom to vomit. I look in the mirror to make sure that my smile is the right one, before I go back out there. This is my house. This is my home. I feel Chinua in my blood when I say, "Tragedy begins when things leave their accustomed place."[3]

We all pile into a car and go to the graveyard to pay our respects to my deceased great-grandfather. And the visit is fairly short, as we tend to the dead man's home by tearing away weeds from the ground surrounding his head, as if maybe he will be more comfortable now. And we leave him a smoke at his gravestone for later that night, when darkness gains dimensions and the white in the sky beats his eyes into repulsion. He will have something to remember us by, one night less painful. And when we all progress into the car, once more, I wonder if this mosquito that's been circling my face since I've arrived here is the dead man, trying to get a full view of the fruits of his labor.

I still remember it, as clearly as if it were yesterday. We drive up to a beautiful white house, surrounded by a picket fence that designates property lines. On the left side there is a pecan tree that's been eyeing me since I set foot on the property. And then to the southeastern part there is a grapevine, white and green and purple; they smile at me, knowing that I'll be over for a visit later. We step inside and everything is modern, every channel imaginable on the television, and I smile and I lie back on the recliner and I know that this is where I was meant to be. A Southern belle, amongst my other Southern folk, eating pecan pie and drinking grape juice from the vine in my back yard, while my accent seduces Northern boys. All the while, my mind stays at home, in bed, awaiting the night when I can look up in the sky and not feel contempt for the stars that spit nasty pellets of white, bright light in and out of my beautiful sky, that I've never seen in its purest form.

Some call me pro-black. I call myself confused, a wanderer in a world where everyone is one-half this, and one-fourth that, and one-eighth the other. I stand alone underneath an apple tree and the truth is that I am the result of slavery. I do not know my ancestor that immigrated to America. But I will tell you that he/she/it did not want to come. This I know because all of those in my family are like me. We feel the same things. We think the same things. We breathe the same recycled tears. And knowing that I would never leave the most beautiful place on earth, where animals beat down on the land and, in turn, the land pushes up upon them and everything is mutual, to come to this place where the scales of justice are tilted three-fifths in favor of the devil's hands. Knowing this, I know that I am the result of many fights and battles and struggles and tears left to rot inside human souls, untouched, unheard. Call me what you will, but you will have to call me something, because I will not go nameless. I am screaming for those that I have no name to connect with. Call me something, because I won't let you live your life happily while I sit here bearing this burden, which makes my back cramp and my shoulders stiff and my heart cold. I will never let you forget, because I will not go forgotten. You only stand as tall as you do because you are standing atop my ancestors' backs. And I am only as strong as I am because I am the compilation of their failed endeavors, misplaced emotion and forgotten, nameless history. I am the compilation that is feared as, similarly, I fear the world. Call me what you will, but don't call me African-American, because I was stripped of that a long time ago, to the point where I can no longer look my fellow man in the eye and greet him as such. Maybe he is my relative. Who has done this hideous regression on my people? I look at you in the mirror and I smile at you while I try to forget these things that I never knew, but know.

174

Nobody knows what it feels like to live in my world, with not too much darkness because street lamps light the way, so that little girls, traveling home after long days at school and nights on the neighbor's porch, won't have to be scared walking in back alleys, near city dumps, where rats and roaches make themselves at home. With death and disease and children being born to babies all around me, this is where I am most comfortable. I live this life, of Metrocards, of EZ Pass, of jeans crumpling across, over and through track runners' legs and touch football games on paved streets on dead-end blocks. With soul food Thanksgivings and Christmases in houses where Jesus has never come to pay a visit, I wonder where's the glue that binds these misshapen puzzle pieces. But after a while, I stop analyzing and prophesying and just sit back and watch the game with a fried wing-fling in my hand and I pretend that I'm not worrying about when I have to go back to school, in a nice, quaint, petite New England suburb. I worry about the fun that I'm missing because I am not with my classmates, and then I worry what would my relatives say if they knew how I pronounced words when speaking to these friends, when I sit at my desk, in my nice little dorm room, in this quaint little dorm, in this petite little New England suburb. And then I relax once more and I let my own self-consciousness seep out of my pores and I give up and give in to cholesterol and high blood pressure-provoking food, which has always meant love in my house. And day in and day out I wonder why people look upon my paradise as a ghetto, with mis-guided souls trapped within the confines of misfortune and poverty and negroism and ebonics. And I can't escape my need to be here, amidst this love that only a dying breed can possess.

Now as my leg falls asleep under the weight of this computer, which has already passed out under the weight of my words, I won-der if I have said what I meant to say. If these words here are actu-ally what my soul feels or if my knowledge of history and bad personal experiences and unclaimed pain and situations misunder-stood have finally concocted this burst of red and orange flames,"burning bright"4 inside a part of me that I haven't named yet. My body tells me that I've cried enough for one day and that I should go to bed, and rest up. Because as simple as it seems, things in this life "do not go gentle."5 Each time I look up, I see these bright lights that I've always thought to be unwanted specks in a landscape much greater and much more beautiful than any that my eyes have ever seen. These lights that make me want to cry, because I can't hold the weight of the world and the weight of the world beyond the world upon these two human shoulders. I want to give up and just go to bed, without having fully explained myself, because now I know that when something has lived within you for so long, you can never get it out in a form that others who can't relate, can comprehend. It is one thing to know something and it is another to understand it. And I've been telling you things that you already know, but now I don't understand my own thoughts.

So I dream little Kente Cloth dreams of lands far away, sitting on desolate, dry sands, bearing fresh grapes and pecans to place on the table of my poverty-stricken family, that can't see the beauty of the night, because city lights emit contaminated fumes across life itself. But all is not lost as we watch innumerable channels on the television and convene underneath a night sky that tomorrow will bear beautiful pinks and purples and blues and white clumps that will no longer offend me as I walk upon my native land, bearing beautiful colors deriving from fruits of the earth. I walk barefoot upon land that, as I press down on it, pushes up upon me. And I smile, with a tear sliding down my left cheek, and know that my contemplation is not in vain, because this compilation is the most beautiful one that I know of. This is me giving birth to a half African-American, half African child and looking down on her and knowing that she will forever be mine. She will always know her worth. Never will she be raped as I have been.

[1] *Zaragoza, Spain*
[2] *OutKast, Aquemini*
[3] *Chinua Achebe*
[4] *William Blake*
[5] *Dylan Thomas*

Amy Kenna

Inside the City

You wake up one morning;
you realize that you are a city. The sprawl
of your naked limbs
resembles Philadelphian suburbs,
withholding that same self-perpetuating
purpose of existence.
You turn a wrist, realize that your
inner weave of arteries, veins
is a highway system for the
freighters, the locomotives, the buses.
You realize that your intricacies,
like New York subway tunnels,
are simply mechanisms serving
to increase efficiency within
the structure.
You realize that your ruby blood
is nothing more than capital—
capital produced by one single
state-owned factory, central and monopolizing,
hissing with the production of
endless identical items, each
prepared for the market of a million
red and white consumers.
You begin to worry.

Then you walk the city streets,
observe the details of the metropolis.
You notice late-night jazz scenes,
schools of dance and theatre,
underground newspapers, glowing streetlights.
You realize that somewhere
inside the machinery of your organs,
a romantic café is opening its doors.
A public meeting is being held.
An abstract painter in his studio apartment
overlooking Times Square
is visited by inspiration.

You explore your empty streets
at dawn, and take note
of that moment when the sun streaks
over the buildings' tops, when the neighborhoods
unfold like night roses, and
turn open their faces to a thousand
external possibilities.

And then you
stop worrying.

Alison Stine

Passage

They say that my generation
will be the first one
to have less
than our parents;
which means I have been robbed
of saying,
"We never had that when I was young,"
because if we have less,
then what is left for our children
but nothing?

I feel like a little girl
caught playing dress-up in her mother's closet,
her small body lost

in oversized clothes,
stumbling
in shoes too big to fill,
her hands upturned,
palms raised,
begging
for forgiveness.

Alison Stine

Stranger

Someday
I will be free and loud
and beautiful
the same way
I am now hiding
in oversized sweaters,
never raising my hand,
just to prove I can be someone
else.

An old woman is somewhere
inside my stillness,
no makeup,
gray-brown hair stringy down my back
like a witch's broom.
Gray face,
gray eyes
still searching myself
for some sign of recognition.

Bruce Morris

Revelation

Are you pulling the limestone brick yourself
    To build the temple of conformity?

Stand in the Tornado.

Grab the Cobra by the fangs,
    Suck the poison and call it nectar.

Show people that you are the weed
    In the field of righteousness.

Be the snake in the sleeping bag,
    The sleeping bag of government.

We are the only ones who can show our fathers
    Their syphilis-infected dreams.

It is up to us to suck the bacteria and pus
    From the wounds.

Be the oak tree in the combine's path,
    Take notice of the corn it rolls over,
        Know that you don't have to be popcorn.

Mia Alvar

Lemons

A little taste of lemon,
like honey,
is best as a surprise.
The blinding yellow headed for your face
like a sudden punch,
a small sour stamp on your tongue
drawn back as soon as it came,
a little butterfly
flittering away, much too pretty
to stay.

Lemons are moments,
brief glimpses of shimmering skin
batting eyes coyly
from behind the commonplace green leaves,
a mean little tease, another
"just a little" need,
"just a little" lemon
in your cup of tea,
"just a little" lipstick
before you're sixteen.

Before I was sixteen
I was cute and accidental.
Once I grabbed
a lemon-yellow crayon,
scribbled a hasty little message
of love, and watched the boy
whose desk I stuck it in.
His face scrunched up
as if he tasted every word—
bright, sour, blinding.

Notes like that, they end
after second grade, and
words never come
like sparks
again.

Nora Lawrence

Headlights

The lights from the FDR Drive streak by
outside the window tonight.
I try not to focus my eyes, wanting the double lines of bright white
to continue across to the panes;
two long headlights beaming dependably until sunrise.

And I wonder again how many times you've passed my building,
gone down this highway on your way home, or up it
on your way to school in the morning
and if you've counted stories, and located my window
        from the outside
(my silhouette dancing, a sole shadow shining through the curtain)
or maybe you forget to, now that we've lost touch.

From the brand of each car I can guess who's inside,
whether they're going somewhere in Manhattan
or passing through on the way to Queens.
I convince myself that not only the driver is inside
I don't want anyone to be alone.

Across the lanes the river churns
forming craters and mountains of opaque water
currents are crashing, colliding.
In the dark
everything we see is black and white.

Waking up and looking out again at 4 am—
no one is driving these cars
they slide along the Drive effortlessly
the asphalt shining like liquid black glass

they're not thinking about me.

Lauren Argintar

One More Page in Insincerity

inspired by Susan Gott

could i be read if i was see-through
or would you just see my metal cording
spine, crooked from where you last tried
to "break me"? you wanted to fold me like
a reminder and keep me in your back
pocket. but my skin would not crease,
i was too young then. instead you settled
for a picture and the emulsion tore as
the folds mangled me in your wallet. the
edges frayed. "A little rough around the edges,"
you'd smile, showing me how you still had it,
that you had held on to it for so long.
i'd just look at you wide-eyed and grin with
perfect serenity, my teeth gritting in agreement.
it was the metaphor you always missed.

Vanessa Kogan

Finding the Sky

1.

I've found that small piece of sky between
        the two roofs—I've needed it
now that I can't seem to get thrown into poems—
I've been too busy deciding what is beautiful, what is important
enough to be beautiful
        and I am red-faced, uncontainable: I've decided
        real beauty should make
                you feel
        idle
As though you have to throw yourself into something
        and the sky's the only place that could hold you
and the sky's the only thing you can see easier
                than the ground.
I think of shrinking into myself again but I catch this and look
                up as though I could fall *out*—
        I'm always afraid of "falling into things"
        like the heart is a well.
I have become some symbol for falling,
        throwing my head back and asking the stars
or the ceiling
        to "send me someone";
becoming another person who compares
        time to rivers.
I could count the twelve hundred seconds
                that make up hours if I listened
to the cricket in my dining room singing its lazy drone
                dry-paper wings rubbing in beat with the second hand—
something about his delicately domestic existence is important
                the way we never notice what is constant
                and always forget it's the sun that burns.

I will never forgive clouds
        for their flimsiness.

2.

I read this story about a boy
                who was always escaping on trains
because he liked it when they made the same sound
                his anger made in him
when it was grinding against his box-car belly—
                               I am thinking about this as I watch
                               her and how her small body
                               is so important to me now—perhaps
                               important enough to be beautiful—
                               She is contained, I think, something
                               in her is heavy and filling her out,
                               she can remember what it was like
                               to have been whole;
                               I can remember the night she and I
                               and other well-enough-acquainted girls
                               were slashing the silky cold December air
                               in the every-house-is-the-same neighborhood
                               throwing off our shirts and pushing our
                               chests out as we ran
                our breasts bouncing like our kicking limbs
                    nipples hardening in the cold
as if preparing to meet the ocean
                               and not the muted air.
Under the grainy lights of street lamps
                we found our sweaters for each other—
This is yours I said.
                               In the great dispersion of summer
                               her father
                               killed her mother
                               while she was in the house;
                               We all found out separately
                               and stayed separate about it,
                               all the time wondering just how to come
                               together—
                               When I tried to think of the sounds
                               that could
                               have possibly been inside of her,
                               I could think of nothing but trains
                               and how their metal axles
                               start their orbit slowly around the black wheels

186

and then seem to throw themselves *faster, faster,*
until they are silver whirs above the tracks.
Trying to imagine silence, or rather noiselessness—wouldn't silence
itself be so much quieter if only
we were comfortable in it? not like our tight hands
endlessly folding over themselves, ordering to tell life in straight lines
and every week say Amen.

3.

I remember only the air outside the stadium
    that day, when I squinted the sun split into
    pointy rays and I could see the dust under car wheels
    shine like the earth itself was sweating
My father moving rapidly to the train—
    he is too thin to ever be hot or cold—
leaping on at 125th Street,
    the train moved like a wounded snake out of the Bronx
    lifting the hair off my neck and draping it over the seat,
    feeling the leather headrest like a huge leech clinging to my nape.
I remember I could feel the skin on my forehead
    buckle, where a pimple was forming, and I knew that
    I would bleed the next day, and it would be heavy like the
    trawling cars and
    as thick as my throat walls opening to accept the viscous
    swallows of breath and diesel.
Turning to watch the thin reflection of
    my face on the glass
    as it skidded against
    the night's strange pointillism of lighted windows—
I said to my father *why don't you grow a mustache, like when I was born,*
and with the newspaper still over his face, he answered me,
    because it's just extra baggage.
And that was the first time I thought
    of all the people I could have called father but didn't
    because I can't belong to that many people—
At home that night was the same as this night,
    safe in its ungiving loyalty: to never give me sleep before
    I imagine sinking into you
    the way I settle into Y-shaped branches;
    my hair splayed over the pillow, I think of tomorrow, when I will
have to ask my mother to braid my hair
        because I hate wearing it long and loose when it's dirty
        and I can't see far enough down my back
        to lock the strands together.

Jesse Dalbacka

Four Pieces of Transition

1. Dreaming is a spectator sport

I had a dream the other night. In it, my parents were yelling at each other in a way I know they are capable of doing, but never do. I don't know how it is, exactly, that I know they are capable. But I know the way my mom's mind analyzes personal things. It knits and purls itself into a row of stitches. Sometimes, all that knitting adds up to a sleeve, but you'll never catch her wearing her heart on it. She keeps too many things to herself. My dad works at relationships like the natural carpenter he is. Measure twice, cut once, but hard. Use short words like heavy blows from hammers, driving to the point of splintering. After ten years, they still don't work together. They just run parallel. Bodies in motion will stay in motion. That seems to go for the unhappier ones, too. But this all comes with the after-dream analysis. I couldn't explain this to them in the dream. I've found there are very few soliloquies in my subconscious.

2. Being necessarily distracted

So, my mom and dad were yelling at each other. Nonstop. Finally, because it was tiring, or maybe because it was Thanksgiving, I interrupted. "If you two can't quit, I'm going off to college, and I'm never coming back." This part I remembered in the morning, even after I had washed from my face the layers of sweat, hot from the room, cold from the dream, now dried. And, even after I was out the door, fed, and caffeinated, I thought about it. A lot. This was a problem for two reasons. **A.** I had just turned one of both my and my mother's most pressing fears into a threat. Something considerable, permanent, uncomfortable, like a tattoo. A tattoo is kind of like leaving, it's something easy to do on impulse. You just move your body through the door. I wonder when I will ever drop the stigma that turning eighteen means that right decisions will start making themselves. Not until nineteen, probably. Then, reason **B.** The realization that this is a large fear of mine. Maybe things at college will be too good for me to come back often, or even regularly. Supposedly, that's growing up, which is all I've ever really wanted to do, which means I don't have to feel bad. So now I'm walking around, feeling bad about not really feeling bad. And still not knowing what to do.

3. Senseless violence or recurring themes

The dream progressed, and it was nearly time to eat. Finally, after 18 years, there was room for me at the adult table. But that meant that I had to slaughter, pluck, cook, and do whatever else it is you have to do to a goose to make it edible. We have never eaten goose. I'm not even sure who in my family likes goose. But, I had to do it. It kept playing dead, then running away when I would set it down on the cutting board. Secretly, I was glad that I didn't actually have to chop its neck. I imagined the sound to be a barbarian ripping or shredding noise. The sick crack of snapping into a primordial Slim Jim. Maybe that was why Peter Pan never grew up. His family switched to geese, too. My uncle was getting mad. "You're supposed to be a good cook!" he yelled.

"But I don't kill geese," I yelled back. I don't remember what happened after that. Mostly, I was disappointed that I couldn't trade places with the goose. It would have been nice to have my neck laid out for me, my head taken off like a bitter stem and left alone in the compost heap. But that doesn't happen at the adult table. Every mature person who is any mature person takes responsibility for their geese still running around the house.

4. Negative gravity and other forces

I used to have a lot of those falling dreams. I'd tumble out of cars. Windows. Balconies. Through floors. I'm always trying to disentangle blame from being out of control. Sometimes, there is no push or pull, you just fall. Landing is only a starting point. It's always been important that I pick myself up. But, I do it a lot unnecessarily. I mean, I'm trying to pick myself up more times than I am falling. I don't know what this does to a person, what sort of balance it gives them. What is the opposite of falling, is it flying?

Jesse Dalbacka

When the Woman Is Contemporary, and the Kitchen Belongs to Someone Else

1. Every day, I would ponder the dangers in being a cook. It's not so monotonous as you think, I would tell myself. There are no floor mats, I could slip in a puddle of cream sauce. I could open the oven door and lose my eyebrows from the heat. A doctor told me once that eyebrows usually don't grow back. That could mean permanent disfigurement, a visit to a specialist, and so on. I felt better having such a supposedly dangerous job. I could lose my life at any moment. Sometimes, this pondering would distract me, and I would cut myself. I think standing on my feet for so long thinned my blood. It would run everywhere. Blood and grease are two things you can never wash out of an apron. No one understood why I would clean out my cut and laugh. But this was similar to a lot of mistakes I made that summer. Good cooks don't ruin sauces. They don't burn soups or add too many spices to a dish. They also don't cut themselves. You learn how to not do these things. And you pour your failures down the sink. I'd watch my blood swirl in the steel basin like a bad batch of whipped cream and think, if only I had stiff peaks, I wouldn't have to throw this away.

2. Every place has its own atmosphere thickener. Clubs have smoke. Lumberyards, sawdust. Kitchens have spices and herbs. I might come home smelling of cilantro, basil, tarragon, garlic, just this mess of pungencies no one would want to taste or, certainly, savor. I do not like the smell of curry, but it hung around. Had more tenacity than most flavors. Certain smells, certain people are difficult to ignore. Like my boss. Jailbait, he called me. I would shrink, or the walls would shrink, or both. Suddenly, there would be big stoves, huge pans, humongous knives, and a tiny me. It was like sharing a full-size bed with a kicker. It doesn't seem right to blame. It's easiest to just roll over, save space by turning inside yourself. I still can't eat curry because it is what I imagine older men to taste like.

190

Jeffrey Chiu

Perfect Pitch

This talent for perception
     for effortless familiarity
for hearing supermarket jingles
     in cheerful Cs and Gs
with certainty, you sift out
     D-sharps, A-flats, Bs,
from a song's blend of notes
     which seem to me
unharmonious at best.
     Some have this gift
of sense, some do not.
     I always thought of it
as vision, a piano in your head,
     keys playing themselves,
an invisible deity revealing
     a secret only to you.
Years ago, we passed a church
     and heard its bells toll.
You said they sounded slightly
     out of tune. I listened
and heard nothing peculiar,
     then realized how deaf
I was and how many must share
     my condition, born into
accepting what we hear.
     So much sounds valid:
rush hour traffic, the dog barking,
     thunder at sunset.
Perfection unrecognized
     is just another noise.

Alexis Goldberg

Tory Sitting on a Couch in a Coffee Shop on the Corner of Ninth Street and Avenue A

with a coffee that she announces will make her hands shake later
Tory is sitting on a couch in a coffee shop on the corner of Ninth Street
      and Avenue A
and she is talking on a cell phone that isn't hers

and as I am watching her talk on the phone the way that her mouth
      moves catches my eyes
I never noticed before the way that her lips close over every word
and the way that her d's and t's are crisp like lettuce

Tory is one day older then me
and she is the kind of person you'd like to see in silhouette
to photograph with barely any background and only a void Tory
and you can imagine her outline contrasted against a light sky:
        pug nose, curly hair
        like an angelic baby faced Medusa
        eyelashes protruding from her profile
        so long they push their way out of the darkness
        the only individual part of the well-crafted blur

and as I am watching her talk on the phone I imagine what it would be
      like to have Tory as a best friend
to have that buoyant laugh on the other end of the phone
to see her every Friday night
to spend that 16-year-old cliché with her
where we eat Ben & Jerry's and lament loves lost

and as I am watching her talk on the phone I am wondering what it
      would be like to be Tory
to be all blonde curls, I am wondering if she ever feels like an overgrown
      Shirley Temple, or a
junior Miss America, with her smile so wide, and I am wondering what
      it would be like to have
the bluest eyes I've ever seen, and to have her air of orange juice and
      freshly cut grass, and I am
wondering what it would be like to be a bad girl in a good girl's persona.

and Tory hangs up the phone, and holds up her hands,
      "did you see when I was talking on the phone," she says,
      "did you notice anything?"
and I say no
and she says,
      "my hands were shaking."

Emily Parker

Poised

Poised is a word often synonymous with
able-bodied, it's that same shuteye
feeling of being just
waiting at a stop street

Clenched wings (and teeth) are facets of this
early imagination, bumps and
grinds smoothed over by passing traffic so your
one core holds compact and ready, willing—

until people say you have the body of a dancer

Jessica Bulman

Dead Moths

There are dead moths in the bathroom
I say it as if it were a simple fact
worn smooth by time—
as if this had no implications
beyond itself
and I were not standing here
dripping water, writing it—
as if their crushed
brown and white speckled wings
their ribbon torsos
held truer than the butterflies
we used to make with our hands
hooking the thumbs
waving the fingers.

I dreamed I was flying
high beyond the last billowing tree
towards the etiolated moon
shedding streamers
through the night sky—
I waved my wings, these two hands
of bone and flesh
and tried to keep myself
above the oaks and maples
leaves mottled like wings.

The moths come every year at this time
to invade the sink and scatter
their paper wings
their paper clip antennae
on the toothpaste and soap
I held a wing pinched between my
forefinger and thumb with
the tenderness and delicacy
of handling an infant
to show respect for the dead.

But when last night I tried
to keep myself above the trees
with my butterfly hands
I fell lower and lower
until I woke to find
moths in the bathtub
wings drowned
hunched and clinging to themselves
like flowers in a drought
and then as I turned the faucet
one flew away.

Mark Tanno

Bright Snow Cold

Out into the bright snow cold,
The wind sweeps around a drumcan fire—
The mouth of night swallows me whole.

Black, frozen rivers roll and unfold
In the backwash of cities; large liquid stars
Stream out into the bright snow cold.

My face a nugget of coal
Lit by fires on barges, the junked pier.
The mouth of night swallows me whole.

I've sold
My final breath as a streetside flower. I'm bare
To the bright snow cold.

I've folded
Time into a small cancer.
The mouth of night swallows me whole.

On the slow water, the creeping lull,
The husk of winter.
Out into the bright snow cold,
The mouth of night swallows me whole.

Jenny Jones

Chestnut

You've got your cheek pressed to the window. The twentieth of October air has chilled the glass and when it touches your skin it takes your breath away. But it gradually eases and you breathe more easily. You feel your lungs fill with fresh air when, all around you, you sense the smoky bus air play around the figures who act out this daily scene. They call it "going home."

You don't want to play with them today. The glass shows the fields fade into the distance beyond the no smoking sticker on the window. The autumn is almost over and it's taking the last hazy light with it, and you sigh because you want it back.

You put a hand into your coat pocket and find a chestnut. Its shiny oiled surface sleeps in the palm of your hand and begins to awaken memories of the autumns before. You can hear piles of parchment leaves, the green smell they emitted as they decayed to gold. Every weekend you tramped in hat and scarf and took a Safeways bag, fresh from Byres Road that morning. Your mum had given you it, faithful that you would fill it with chessies. There was this one chessie, size of an apple. You had found it. Right down by the railing where the Botanics met Great Western Road. Car fumes in the haze and a ray of sun falling on the leaves. You'd shrieked with delight, imagining the size of the chessie inside. Your brother cried because he hadn't found one yet. And because it was cold. But when you opened it, you did it carefully with Dad's penknife. You never threw them, that made a mess. There was no giant chessie, only four little ones. But there they were nestling in the apple-white flesh, their skins so oily and smooth. You never thought about the day they'd dry up and the veins would push to the surface of a wrinkled and dulled skin.

You never thought of the day that you wouldn't be able to do that anymore. Looking out the window there isn't a chessie tree in sight, only those Scandinavian plantation firs. Christmas trees. You never liked Christmas. You can see the smoky haze drifting down into the valley. The distance is blue. The distance is happy houses. Little houses in the country. They have a common balance. They work their hardest, they love families, wives, husbands and kids. They have salaries and are appreciated for what they give the world. Here you are somebody who has promise, who has all the best chances. You are fortunate, they think you'll go far.

But I still wanted to take you back to the leaves with your Safeways bag. I can't, though, I can only preserve what you collected there in vinegar and leave it out to dry and wrinkle in the closing of the sunshine.

Jenny Jones

Millstone

The air smothered me. The bus home was hot and I felt like I wasn't there. I wasn't part of it. Somebody had taken my mind and put it somewhere. Somewhere else. This wasn't a new feeling. It was an everyday occurrence. Like a safety catch. Home was the same as it usually was. Chaotic. I'd be okay, though. I'd just shut myself in my room for a while with my music and I'd block it out. They say that crazy people don't know they're crazy. Maybe they're wrong, or maybe it's just me. Because I'm painfully aware that I'm distancing myself from...what, I don't know.

Later, the phone rang. For me. Anna wanted to know if I was okay. Apparently I seemed "messed up." Silence. I wanted to tell her I didn't know. I felt that I owed her something, but for some reason...I couldn't. Like, she wouldn't get it. So I just uttered some sound and we arranged to meet later on, in the park.

It was colder now than it had been all week. Anna was waiting for me. She was on the seesaw, calling at me to get on the other end. I stuffed my hands into my pockets. She ran after me and we walked in silence, not really knowing where to. Till we got to the river. The perfectly still, calm, clean river water smelt good. The stone bridge glinted like a diving...board. My mind raced past everything that had been weighing down on me and my footsteps were ticking like water dripping on the stone. I climbed onto the stone wall and everything was clear. I could hear the flies buzzing over the water, tree leaves rustling, I could hear the bugs that called through the leaves. I could smell the smoke from the sleepy chimneys behind me. The grass in the park. The birds in the sky. I could taste metal. I could see the fish darting under the surface of the water, the clouds that weighed like millstones above me. I could see Anna's frozen face.

I jumped. My feet landed on the bridge and didn't give up their wings until I knelt by the riverbank, untying my laces. All around me the grass grew like a jungle, zooming in on me inch by inch each millisecond I wasted on the bank. I stood by the edge, gathering posture and launched myself away from the world, towards the water.

I'd heard it said that water was the source of all life, the purest thing we need, worshipped through the ages...it's true. Under the water, I made out shapes of stones through the muddy water and felt my hair dance as vines around my head. Surfacing, I could see Anna calling from the bank, she shouted that I was daft, but she was untying her shoes too. Water makes you weightless. It also makes the millstone around your neck weightless.

Caroline Hagood

Core

The way I want that which is clutter and that which is emptiness
With equal passion
Threatens to slice me down the middle
Create a bodily civil war—
Under all those layers of bodily things
Riot my body radicals
My fire in all this river
My shame, my pride, my core

And in this state I ask
Is confusion really my core?
Is it at the gate to the rest of me
Waiting to release
The Ambivalence All-stars
The anaconda of the mind
Destroying that which is doubt-weakened
By the natural selection of belief
My simmering pot of decisions

And in this state I ask
Where the balance lies
Where the blanks touch
Connected by way of the below-water route
The official spot of the in-between
The unsteady

Lindsay Washick

Petal

There was some sort of music playing against some sort of background and it was soft and it felt good. Here's to nothing; to everything I thought I was and brief endings at the close of the night. A quick note or two. Before the sun comes up and the light goes out. Before something in your life makes sense and everything falls to pieces as it usually does, at least in mine. Finally, the test to see if I can stay that strong. A dollar to say that I will. A petal...there was nothing there all along.

Alexis Goldberg

I Had to Stop

I had to stop today, on the way home from school, and check my
reflection in the rearview mirror of a dusty blue station wagon.
I wiped the mirror off twice, and blackened my fingers, looking for
    some sign that I had aged.
Something I might not have noticed since I last looked in a mirror,
    something that might have been changed
in an application of lip gloss or an unbuttoning of my coat, showing
    the way my necklace hits my neck.
I looked for something of that sort that might have changed me.
I couldn't find it, though.
I was certain it would be there but I couldn't find it.

On the way home, before the mirror, I had stopped on Prince Street
    to admire a painting of some unknown street peddler.
I looked and he told me that the painting I was regarding was the
    third in the series, that they were in consecutive order.
So I saw them all through and I really did like them, all of them,
    and not in that sort of obligatory way you
feel you have to compliment the artwork on the street because the
    artist took time out to talk to you, either.
I liked them a lot and I told him so.
He asked me if I was an art student and I said no, just interested,
    and do you paint or draw at all, he asked
and I thought of my figure-drawing class two periods a week and I
    said yes I draw, sort of, yes I do.
Then he asked me where I went to school and I said Saint Ann's, it's
    in Brooklyn, right over the bridge.
He said what sort of a place is that and I must have looked puzzled
    so he said is it a university?
No, said I, oh no, it's just a high school, so what are you he asked, a
    senior or a junior or what year you in I mean.
And I thought about it and all of a sudden I wanted to be old and I
    wanted someone to think I was old, or
older, anyway not quite so young, and I looked down at the ground
    and met his eyes and said I'm a junior,
and he said you're so young and I can't even remember my junior
    year anymore, he looked down at his
paintings and said you must have been born around the time I was

doing these, what year were you born in?
So I thought fast and said '80 I was born in 1980, as though there
   might be some confusion as to the century.
He said that's just the year I was finishing this last one, this
   last painting here.
It was the one about rebirth and I felt this sudden connection between
   me and this struggling artist I had just
met, who was painting about birth the year I was born and then I
   remembered I wasn't born in 1980 at all
and I felt stupid, and I said well anyway your paintings are lovely and
   thank you very much and walked away.
Then I checked the mirror in the station wagon but only after I was
   out of eyeshot.
I couldn't figure out why I didn't look older.
Someone had just thought I was a college student. I expected to have
   grown, if even subtly, but I hadn't.
Not in that station wagon.

Walking home with dirty fingers I thought
perhaps the guise of maturity disappeared when I lied about my age.

Beth Herskovits

Witch

My family is in the business of magic. We live in a purple house where my older sister Mikale and I share the attic. My mother is a fortune teller.

Before he lost his job and we moved to Arizona, my father was a chef in TriBeCa, New York City. That was nearly three years ago. Now he has his own restaurant, the Psychic Café; he's in business with my mother.

The Psychic Café is separated from the purple house by a wall. We used to waitress together, Mikale and I, but now it's just me. Mikale quit because of some boy and I've been getting paid: which is more than fair, working the double shift.

It was while waitressing that I met Hazel Corren. She was with a guy in a leather jacket and when I came around to ask them how their food was, he burped twice. That was after he spilled soda on the table, after I had to send over Sam the busboy to clean up. They didn't leave a tip.

Our family business is in the mountains, outside Sedona. We were even reviewed in the local papers. They came to our house and took our picture; I was in it and Mom and Dad. Mikale sat out. She didn't even come out of her room, but I was quoted.

"The Café is great for people my age, too," I said. "Lots of kids from my school come here on dates."

When the paper finally came out, three of my teachers cut out the article for me, asking if I had seen it. Mom hung a framed copy in the café. Mikale said, "I could die."

Hazel came up to me in the school parking lot after seeing the article. "I saw the paper," she said, in a forward sort of way. She squinted her eyes. "You deserved it. Your parents, I mean." She paused. "The food was really good," she continued generously. She had a silver armband clasped around her upper left arm. "I dumped him, you know," she said, as if in explanation. As if that information was reason enough for her to be standing where she was with me standing where I was.

I think I laughed.

Hazel promised to stop by the café sometime. While she said it, she pushed her blonde hair behind her ears with both hands. I think I smiled.

I once asked Mom if she could really see the future. Mikale, sitting next to me at the kitchen table, snorted in response. Three years ago, Mom was a high school guidance counselor, she said. In case I'd forgotten.

Mikale tells me about Reed at night in the attic. She grumbles then. All her hates. "If only," she says. If only we had stayed in New York. If only.

I tell Mikale that I want to hear what happened. Between her and Reed, her first Arizona boyfriend. She was fifteen, I was thirteen, and it was nearly three years ago; we had barely even settled in. Reed was older, a junior, and he had older friends: girls with Jeep Wranglers and cigarettes, guys with beepers and silver dog collars. This is how Mikale described them: the kids from Scottsdale, where they have money.

"Well," she says. "Reed just didn't take well to the purple house or to Mom's silver toga and turban uniform, either." She says it with her eyebrows raised.

It was because of Reed, I guess, that Mikale quit her waitressing job. We don't bring friends home anymore either; I learn from Mikale. After Reed she acted a little extreme, maybe, but for me, at least, it pays well.

* * *

There's a sign outside the Psychic Café. A light blue and silver one which hangs from a wooden, upside-down "L" in our front yard. Hazel, who I haven't seen since the parking lot, is standing by the sign, swinging it back and forth between her hands, when I get off from work. I don't say anything but kind of wrinkle my nose at her. "If you were going to run away from home," she says, "What would you take?"

"My flowered sundress," I answer immediately. "It's my favorite. And money, probably."

She nods. "To buy food, yeah. Actually I was wondering if the café is open."

It isn't, so I set her up on the floor of my attic with cereal and cookies. "What would you take?" I ask. "If you were running away, I mean?"

"A map," she says. Then she giggles. "I mean, I think it would be a good idea for me to have one."

"If you were going far," I say. "Then you would need one."

"I'd go to New York," Hazel says, rolling onto her stomach. "Where the witches live."

"The witches live in New York?"

"Isn't that where you're from?" she says and sits up abruptly. "How 'bout you; where would you go?"

But we weren't witches in New York, I want to say, but Hazel's eyes are trained on mine. "Hawaii," I answer. "But I don't know if I could. Run away, that is."

Hazel plays with her hair. "Oh, I could," she says. "I could definitely." I think that she's the first person who's in my room who would maybe still want to be in my room after seeing Mom as a psychic. So I let her spend the night. She leaves for her brother's house the next morning.

* * *

I ask Mikale about where she and Reed used to go on their dates. She says that, at times, she used to let Reed and his friends, Kris and Sean, come over to our house when she thought no one would be home. At night, she says, the house didn't look as bad. Even still, she says, they called our house a fun house or a haunted house. Even though we bought all our inside furniture in real furniture stores, she says.

"But what did they want to do here," I ask, sitting small in bed with the covers looped around my shoulders. Mikale's hair is glossy black on black in the dark.

"Drink," Mikale says. "Smoke. Sometimes vomit. Eat. You used to comment on the smells in here," she says. "When you came home from wherever you had been with Mom and Dad. Well, now you know."

"Now I know," I say and lie down, staring at the blackness in the corners of the ceiling. " And they were really in here? But they—you kept them on your side, didn't you?"

Mikale laughs. "Kris and Sean once made out on your bed. I didn't even say anything. Reed and I just sort of looked at each other and then Reed took another drink."

"On my bed?"

Mikale's laughter is harsh. "They brought chalk," she says. "To draw on the floor. And, yes, I let them. I let Kris borrow my favorite jeans and cut the legs when they were too long on her. Kris was so little. You could blow on her and she'd float right into the air."

"And she was on my bed? You were joking about that, weren't you, Mikale?"

"Nadine, grow up," she says. "Grow up. You wanted to hear this, you wanted to."

I prop up on an elbow to search for where her eyes are in the dark. Where it is that Mikale's looking.

"Come on," she says. "You washed the sheets and everything. Eventually you did."

"Okay," I say finally. "I wanted to know this."

Hazel is wearing cut-offs the next time she comes by the Psychic Café. Her legs are shiny. "Ready to order, please," she says when I pass by her table. She smiles. Hazel has straight teeth like they do in Scottsdale.

"Where have you been lately?" I ask.

"Around," she says, waving her hand. "Visiting. My brother, my grandparents. Dad's in the middle of his biggest case ever, so he says, and I don't even think he noticed."

"And your mom?"

"She noticed," Hazel says, fingering her fork. "You know, you really do look like a waitress with that apron-thing tied around your waist." She rubs her thumbs down her water glass. "So, where does the famous fortune-teller keep her crystal ball?"

I take a pen and pad out of my apron-skirt and seesaw the pen between two fingers. "See that curtain? There's a room behind it and she's there, waiting for customers to come in on their way out."

"Have you ever seen her in action?" I tell her I haven't. "How come?" Hazel asks, resting her elbows on the table and her chin on her fists.

"I don't know. Mom says she won't take that responsibility," I say. It's a lie; Mom has always said that magic is a business only. You don't want this way of life, she's always said. I press the tip of the pen to the pad. "What'll it be?"

She sighs with an exaggerated raise of her chest. "French fries," she says. She says, "That's too bad for you. I can't wait to see my future in a crystal ball."

Me too, I'm always asking Mom to let me try it, I almost say, but another customer calls for a check somewhere behind me. "We should hang out sometime," I say instead. It's more of an apology than anything else.

"Go, go," she says, making a motion to move me along. She smiles again and shows her Scottsdale teeth.

"It was Kris's idea to have the seance here," Mikale says. "This is the fun house, the haunted house. Nadine, you don't want to hear this," she says, stopping quickly.

"I do," I tell her. I untuck my covers and sit on the foot of her bed. She kicks at me until I move out of reach before she continues.

208

"They brought this music. And candles, aromatherapy you'd call it, they were sweet-smelling. Reed brought a black bulb and Sean brought crystals; they were rocks actually, the colorful kind they sell to tourists. They set up everything and we sat in a circle and Sean wanted to sit naked, but he had another term for it—what was it? Oh yeah, sky-clad."

Mikale is looking down at her hands, I think. It's hard to see in the dark. "Well, did you?" I ask.

Mikale says, "But then Kris turned to me and asked, 'Mikale, what does your Mom wear in the haunted restaurant?' And she wanted to know if she could try it on, Mom's costume. So we all headed downstairs; we could still hear the music even in Mom's bedroom and Sean wanted to know if he could search the drawers for condoms."

I grab onto Mikale's ankle. "Did you let him?" I breathe.

Mikale kicks out of my grasp, knocking her toes against my chin. "I opened Mom's closet," Mikale says. "Where Mom has her silver lamé uniforms. The next thing I knew, Kris was breathing hard and she shook out of her shirt and, right there, started raveling the material round and round her bare stomach. Suddenly, she started laughing and, with Kris still dragging the lamé, we headed back to the attic to wait for midnight. And Reed said, 'Your mother wears that? I didn't know your mother wears that.'"

Mikale is quiet and plays with the top of her blanket. "Is that it?" I ask. Mikale shakes her head. "So who'd you summon? In the seance?"

"Elvis and Vivien Leigh," Mikale says. "Really, Nadine, I don't remember. Kris got to do it. She was wearing Mom's clothes. I had to give directions, though, so I faked something. Was Vivien Leigh the nymphomaniac? Because Sean asked her about that."

"He's perverted," I tell Mikale.

"He is," Mikale agrees. "Most definitely."

She stops. "So what was the big deal?" I ask. "Mikale, what was it?"

Mikale doesn't say anything. I lean forward place my hands near her neck like I want to choke her. It's an awkward hug with our faces so close, foreheads almost touching. She's breathing like she's crying and she's sweating. The back of her neck is wet.

* * *

Hazel calls at eight o'clock in the morning and she wakes me up. "Nadine, do you want to go to the beach?" she asks. No hello even. I'm half asleep and I make her repeat the question.

The beach is not a real beach but an adult-sized sandbox at a nearby Hyatt Regency. Hazel wears a metallic bikini which is like her skin, golden and glossy. Her belly button is pierced.

Hazel and I buy a red plastic pail and shovel and sit in the sand. "You'd miss this in New York," I say. "It's polluted there, you know."

Hazel examines a shovelful of sand in the sunlight. It's flecked with red and silver. "Do you want to know what I'd do in New York?" And she makes me promise not to laugh. "Dance on fire escapes, chanting spells." She spreads her arms.

"Topless?" I ask and I laugh anyway. "Sky-clad?"

Hazel stands up and starts kicking sand in my lap. "Why all the questions, huh, Witch? Come on, Witch, you know the answers, you can tell the future." She's laughing, though. I roll away to protect my eyes and throw sand over my shoulder at her feet. "It runs in the family. I know it, Witch; I can feel your aura." Hazel and I keep flinging sand until the lifeguard comes over and tells us to cut it out. He doesn't say it in a mean way, because it's a nice hotel. Hazel plops down next to me.

"I have sand in my bathing suit," I say.

"Witch," Hazel whispers and giggles.

*　*　*

After she gets home from her summer job lifeguarding, Mikale corners me in the kitchen while I'm eating an apple. "Nice burn," she says.

"Anyone drown today?" I ask.

"Almost but I saved the guy. He was a Tom Cruise look-alike, I swear to God. Afterwards, he asked me to marry him."

"Ha," I say, and take another bite of my apple.

"Alright," Mikale says. "He was close to sixty and afterwards he pinched my behind."

"Liar," I say. "Go shower or something."

"I thought you wanted to know," Mikale says. "About what the big deal was." She leans her back against the sink with her hands curled around the top of the basin.

"Well?"

"That night," she says. "The night of the seance, I stole Mom's crystal ball. It was so easy; I saw where she kept it when I opened her closet. It was in a red box on the rack above her clothes. When I placed my hands on it in the attic, I could see these little lightning bolts flashing around inside."

"Wow," I say. It comes out a whisper.

"Yeah, Kris was floored. She kept wanting to touch it and I wouldn't let her. It was so great, actually, until Mom walked in on us."

"Mom? Mom who's always saying magic is a business Mom?"

"Yeah, wearing this little white dress. Almost a slip. 'You're doing it all wrong,' she said. She started rearranging everything, the candles and the crystals. She sat down right in the circle, right between Kris and Reed. Then she made us join hands and started chanting, like this."

"Mom?"

"Mom," Mikale assures me. "She called on the elements: Earth, Wind, Fire, and Air. She had her hair all loose, not wrapped up in that turban she wears. There was something about her eyes; I can't even describe it. She kept waving her hands. Then she picked up her crystal ball and held it as high above her head as her arms would let her. She tossed it backwards over her shoulders, Nadine, and shattered it to pieces."

Mikale's eyes are wide like she's watching the ball fall. She shudders. "Kris and Sean and Reed, they never came back after that. All because she was afraid I'd grow up to be like her, a psychic who's embarrassed to be a psychic." Mikale is not looking at me.

"It's ironic," I say at last. "One of my friends is convinced that all the magic is back in New York."

Mikale draws a shaky breath. "It was," she says. To which I don't know how to reply.

Hazel comes by the Psychic Café after closing time and she wants to see the future in Mom's crystal ball. "I'll do it," I tell her.

I take Hazel inside the house and upstairs to Mom's bedroom, figuring she'd have something. On the top rack of Mom's closet, I find a red crystal ball box. Hazel reaches in and pats the silver lamé.

I carry the box to the back yard and put it down on the grass behind the restaurant, shaking out my arms.

"Okay," I say. "Give me a few seconds of concentration and then ask whatever question you want." I open the box with what I imagine is a flourish and reach inside to pull out the ball.

"What's wrong?" she asks, when I pull my hands out.

Shaking my head, I empty the box out on the grass so Hazel can see the shards. I think about Mom being embarrassed to be a psychic. Hazel holds a blink for a long time. "Bad magic," she says finally, and sits back on her heels.

Emily Carmichael

Jake

Can't leave for school without me when it's colder
My hands to tie his scarf to pull his sweater
Over his face which looks uncooked and swollen
Like biscuits when my mom forgets the timer
We take the route that goes up past the quarry
The gray wind spins the leaves like wrinkled laundry
It must make him ashamed he's two years older
To cross the street his fingers on my shoulder

And when Clark Avery who plays wide receiver
Whose jacket is unzipped in any weather
Comes gliding up no handed on his Raleigh
A bike I'll buy when I get cash together
He says to me why don't you ditch that loony
I've got ten bucks let's cut and catch a movie
His wheels don't touch the ground he seems to hover
I say to him you watch it he's my brother

Amara Dante Verona

Assembling Bodies

"So you work assembling dolls?" he says.
"No, bodies, I assemble bodies...."
I look out the window, at a tree that embodies
every movement the human form will ever know
from the bend of a lover to the straight of a stranger,
but remains perfectly still, not revealing a thing.
It takes note of my hunched back and heavy eyes, and remembers.
"Girls' bodies mostly, but sometimes young boys too.
There are not enough naturally, and they are always in high demand.
So we make them. My job is towards the end,
you should see them laid out on conveyer belts like virgins.
All of them are beautiful, though, technically, some are flawed.
They are not like mannequins, not that still, flesh could never be confused
with plastic. They lie, as if asleep and waiting for The Kiss—
only, of course, they have no eyes—that is my job.
There are boxes of them: blue, green, brown, hazel.
The coloring is not complex, not like your eyes,
with their seeming blue and surprising flakes of gold, though a shift
of light would force me to describe them entirely different.
I just pop the eyes in the sockets.
And that—*that*—is when they really start to look human."

Natasha Le Bel

Boxing the Female

I saw myself inside again I saw
myself inside a box
which had no bottom, front
nor face only
sides, four, closing
in at right angles and me
crouching low
within the dark
interior
I saw myself inside again I saw
myself a box inside
which kept me as I
grew and grew
too large and round for this or
did the box continue
to shrink and tighten
into a passionate claustrophobia
I saw inside again myself I saw
a box inside myself
I was open
and unclothed without
hair or
shadow to hide my
feminine geometry
which molds and holds
the woman I was then that I am
now
but it was so so dark where it was bare
where I was
uncovered lying undiscovered there
fragile and awkward in the iron emptiness
I began and I
begin
coming out of myself again I am
coming into my form
my born body new and
gravid with musical sensuality
strong and proud

from deep inside this box I am
no longer kept I am no longer
held as precious token beauty
nor quiet prize nor secret pleasure I am
my own ugliness
outside this box this dark hard fist
of walls and corners crushing
my living mind, the blooming
human pattern of my chemistry
through pouring rocks of ferocious silence
that you impose I will
turn over
my bones inside my skin and
shatter these walls with my song I will sing
my ripe real me out loud
with body and heart and brain
all beating against each other
in a heightening passion and I am
opening
this box for you for
myself I am the naked light inside.

Natasha Le Bel

Foot Fire Burn Dance

I do the black boot stomp
on my stucco ceiling
late at night
sometimes
when I think of songs
I write in my head
they beat beat beat up
inside my head breaking
out my eyes and ears
All my winter fever rises
and shoots out through
my pores
to peel the air around me
back and let this new heat expand and
rush
I do the black boot bang
on my thin thin walls
when no one is listening
to crack the paint and
let the music sealed inside
come pouring out
so I can swallow it whole
and in my fury
take it down to my feet and
give it life
I do the black boot thud
on my blue carpet floor
when the fire engines passing by
don't pass
and I hear the sirens
anyhow
I find fire in my feet
beating and burning and
thudding and churning music
out my soles
in my black boot stomp
hard breaking
the angry night

216

VI
Figure It Out

Drew Tarlow

Figure It Out

I remember she told me
you just stick out your
tongue
and make little circles.
It seemed like kindergarten
again: shapes and tongues and
playing around.
And it was all so simple
and happy
as we rolled around
on the wooden floor,
exploring.

Rebecca Alson-Milkman

Sex

I'm going to see him for the weekend
and we play out the scene:
"Do I have anything to worry about?"
"No Daddy," then turn,
smile, check my bag
again for TROJAN-ENZ
extrasensitive with nonoxynol-9 (it's spermicidal—you know) but
now it penetrates:
the absurdity of your question because

You were part of the free love era and
Sure, you had to worry about getting those girls
knocked up
but I'm not just talking pregnancy here.

You never had to approach a partner
request form in hand:
All Former Lovers Please.

By age 20 I'll walk around with a printout:
Column: Name   Column: Date, Hour   Column: # Times He Came

You play the understanding father:
curiosity about the daughter's purity
but this is my
                life
and yes,
it is what you should worry about.

Julia Kate Jarcho

The Glimmerer

You'll meet him soon
the beautiful starry boy, thin as a peapod
and as soft and as reclining
sharp and almost glass because he always leaves
and slips back in again

the mad one with an angel face and head full of light
from all the shadows he's seen
who creeps around stone structures like wind's whisper
behind you, casting fear's fishhooks
into the corner of your eye

he begins to fill in spaces
will you want him there always?
he never talks, just touches
and makes small cuts with his silk fingernails

until you let him have you
so, slicing bright, he makes it dark
as the moon does the sun

coiling around you like an eel
he bites: this is the boy
who brings night on.

Deborah Stein

Heat

hot boys, she says, are sweet in the summertime
muscles burning taut and rippled
steam rising off their shoulders and hanging
in the air, heavy swirling auras of light
and cologne, making a greenhouse in her room

backing away coolly, i say i'm not so sure
with my sour apple gum and dry air conditioning
(keep me from her heat sticking my hand to my cheek
eternal expression of awe) i watch her try
to bloom, bear fruit, or at least create honey
to boil in the fevered friction, wailing as she rubs up
against them and then they stand, patient shiny statues
sweat gleaming just beneath their skin.

Philip Clark

A Hustler Leaves at Dawn

Some days I want
To flee down alleyways,
Running anywhere
Just to feel my feet
Beneath me,
Body in control.

Some nights I think
I'll step away
From the open cars,
Beckoning men,
Restless hours
In hotel rooms.

But I wake
Each morning
At a strange window
Dawn
Greeting me in waves.

When black light
Gives way to gray
I slip away unseen,
Careen through empty streets,
Begging the city
To swallow my steps.

Drew Krewer

Rain

The kids throw rocks at each other, waiting for rain. They wait for mud, for the sloshing of feet in brown water. A giant airplane zooms above the park, the hatch flung open like an unruly mouth. Hundreds of translucent condoms fly through the night air. The kids open their mouths as if to catch them like raindrops. They stick their tongues in them, then place their small fists inside. One by one they put their mouths to the openings and fill them with air; they bat them around like beach balls or thin-skinned balloons.

What are these? one of them yells.

They are fallen angels, says another boy. *See? They have lost their wings.*

They gather the limp bodies in their arms, stuff them deep into their pockets, tie them to their wrists. They run to the lake, dig their knees into the shore, scatter the condoms over the glinting black water. If these angels can't fly, maybe this water—which the clouds and air of heaven will never provide—can float them back home.

Gemma Cooper-Novack

Porn

Nudity onstage
For now, imagine I am Isadora Duncan;
then I can do anything, rip off the red
scarf separating
me from the air; I can imagine it. My body
would be a Greek statue then, paragon; I
would be the free-flowing actor
I've never been, and even bared
for the sky and dirt to see, I could still
stand in triumph, arms extended, stomach
slightly rounded and smooth, eyes
penetrating every member of the audience,
perspective and sweat in the flesh

Nudity offstage
water water water water
silt-shifty sand of tropical shores
almost night almost morning
and me in the center, moon
in and out of clouds, I am embarrassed,
breasts at knees, vagina hidden
in a mist of waves and thighs. It is too bare
here, at three a.m., with people I know and
examination
(I have a friend
who stripped completely in front of six people to prove
that he had no social inhibitions)
it is too beautiful here and I unfold
for a glorious moment, Caribbean fountain
and then sink again into salt sea

The seventeenth annual display of her body
This time it is different.
Suddenly guests attend the exhibition, she no longer
spends the year pinned and wriggling
on an orange wall, suddenly articles
accompany the photo spread. This time
it is different, and she rushes through it in a barrel,
relentless and sightless, wondering where she will land.

Verbal nudity
You
know everything, everything, I
know everything, when we speak, it is all
scraped white with the weight of everything
pressing against the edges, it is almost
pornographic, it is raw and whole, peeled
and shining in Massachusetts night, we laugh as well
and our laughs are woven with secrets
that shimmer between us like silver nets made
for catching deformed moons

Verbal nudity
Now there are seven people for secrets, looser
weave and the same kind of
clothshimmer beauty
(yes, but
like delicate foreign suburbs,
quieter) now among six
or more, I spread everything, everything:
I've given so many pieces at so many times
that I'm never quite certain who knows me whole

Nudity offstage
You all chose strip poker;
it wasn't me. It's simply that
I don't mind losing
five hands in a row, shoes and stockings and
scarf and shirt and bra
and what I do mind
is that you then command me
to put a pillow over my chest

The thirty-fourth annual display of his body
They came together one night,
as love, he showed himself to the woman he
belonged to who belonged to him
over and over, not the first time, but the time
to build the foundation of a child
(over the next years would come a total
of two daughters, love for those and a dissipation
of love for each other, passion
running into the gutters, but of course he didn't
think about that then,
only about the fantasies he'd written letters to her about
and how rapidly
they kept on coming true)

Nudity onstage
Nietzsche bares his genitals
for all to see. We gape and try not to,
try instead to follow
the play where he keeps on saying "I have this part
between my *legs*" in a weeping tone
and the other characters gather around him
we try not to watch only one spot
when the stage is full of focal points
this is such a varied stage

Verbal nudity
Lying in my half-room
together tonight, we share secrets—
not so much secrets
as things that make no sense outside. We talk
about nudity onstage (you would never be naked
in performance, but I would), what it is
that makes us ultimately vulnerable; I say,
well, look at me, look at
how I talk about such things, look
at the way I dress,
it certainly isn't my body

Nudity onstage
We walk past 42nd Street
Porn Palace XXX Video Live Nude Girls
and my companion (she is older,
friend and teacher) says, I went into one of those once,
did I tell you?
Yes, three years ago you told me
how you "got excited. I felt...like I had a dick, you know?"
(it was for research;
for writing a story)
you also told me that no one in those audiences
meets anyone else's eyes

Verbal nudity
There was once a boy who hadn't spoken, who
had silenced the stories of his travels, where
he'd been and all the places he was
afraid to go,
he kept his voice swallowed, his lips
inflexible, sliced at his arms daily
that he might ooze out elsewhere,
until one night
he came inebriated to the telephone, dialed a number
foreign to his fingers; it was midnight
and when a tired voice crept through the receiver
he spilled his voyages to a stranger

The forty-fifth annual display of her body
She's still got sex when she opens the curtains,
but she isn't sure about that
(there are no guarantees),
so Thighmaster Step Aerobics Sweatin'
to the Oldies and then she will climb
into a shimmering dress like the one
she wore twenty years ago and like youth
she will still dance far into the night

Nudity offstage
Peeling off our towels like Astroturf,
flat from neck to knee,
we jump into the pool all four
at once with a voluminous splash,
and swim naked, torsos pale and lean
inside the turquoise water, swimming and splashing
and screaming like maniacs
it is late summer dusk and we
will soon be sticky with chlorine
and there is nothing to hide

Nudity onstage
There was once a girl whose body had almost disappeared;
when she stood alone in the middle of a room it terrified her,
but among others she swathed herself in layers of fabric,
said nothing, remained obscured.
It was only onstage that things were revealed:
with an audience she could hide herself no longer and
people had to wonder for the first time
where she had gone
(I could have asked her sometimes,
but the question would have left both of us
bare backstage in the dim blue light and
I didn't want to do that)

The seventy-ninth annual display of her body
They opened her and found room for
a machine, a hardened clock that keeps her going
attached to her heart;
waking up she could only imagine
what had been done inside her, she found it hard to think
of how deep within her
things could be altered
and how much could be shown

Verbal nudity
Personally,
I don't think I've ever had a problem with peeling down layers.
Even when I am scarred
like imported fruit, even
when I go that deep, I never
mind describing it (at least not here
and not to you) but for you,
every mention of a scar (deeper
than any I have had) is like pulling a copper curtain—
which has dyed your pale skin green
for a long time—
aside

The fifth and eighth annual display of their bodies
They are performers they are fashion
models they are the epitome of glamour stepping
up in the bathtub with water dripping one
of them like a stick and the other
more rounded all covered in soap
bubble dresses, gowns that can
pop or blow away at the slightest
breeze or provocation
giggling, they sing
like tin whistles
and then call for a camera

Nudity onstage
Once my friend went to see a play
(the audience composed
primarily of eighty-year-old women)
where the lights came up and
six buck-naked men started speaking,
on the stage, once I saw a naked performance artist
wearing a box around her breasts,
her partner painting a backdrop upon them
in menstrual blood and once someone
bought my other friend a lesbian
porn video and she watched, fix-
ated and laughing (once someone else decided to watch
a porno with her boyfriend; it was
"close shots of penetration" and it
didn't turn them on at all)

Nudity offstage
There once was a man who lived
in a nudist colony
for seven years at which he met his
future wife;
after two years of courting naked
they eloped and left the colony, settling
down in San Francisco, the edge of the bay;
years later when they were walking
down the street clothed they met a woman they
had known at the colony;
they embraced, said hello—
it was rather awkward

Nudity offstage
There is pre-examination before entering the shower,
always. It is a luxury to find
in the mirror
the torso, the stomach, the pubic
(all the hidden things) assembled—
even when I stood
with four nearly-unknown girls
in a foreign bathroom I did this,
it is the kind of visceral necessity
that is always overlooked

Verbal nudity
Years later, there is still something I miss;
even as I rediscover comfort,
strip off my affectations and plunge
again, I miss walking
into a room with you, or down the street, and knowing
we could take off our clothes at any moment
and nothing would be altered. I read
about the Women Against Pornography movement
of the 1980s; there was a point
when the porn stars
banded together against the movement
and it makes me wonder
the lines are so fine
and there is nothing
like being bare and knowing you are safe

Bob Meyer

Crush

her nervous eyes
reflect warm water
between feet and ceiling
but can she see it?
can she swim?

trunks of elephants
suck the glass
from a slow-moving coffee table
covered by
gnats
algae
and newspaper

the warm water drinks my saliva
my skin
my scream

I'm afraid to look at her
afraid she sees me
sees my scattered brain
with thoughts striped green and orange
thoughts of her
always her

soon elephants will stop drinking
and walk again
will shatter glass coffee table
and see the jungle
not the furniture

Lindsay Washick

Sunday Night

10:48
The hot water hit my skin and washed away tonight's dirt. I loved it

11:08
The cats came out

11:49
At work tonight he didn't know where the soda was. And he didn't
      crush the ice the right way

11:52
He's got big feet. I hear the rain. He told me he loves it

12:00
I wonder if he's working today

Dan Gruenberg

There Is a Girl in the Cafeteria

There is a girl in the cafeteria
that I cannot talk to.

So at night I walk down the hill
into the town, which gives me time to think about things.
And of course she is sleeping,
covers smoothed out by her mother,
while I outwalk my daytime life in a night that shows my breath.

When my path levels I am in town and
walk towards the phone booth outside the gas station.
I place the phone to my ear, but make sure my hand is resting on
the metal piece
which holds the receiver when not in use,
so that even the operator is unaware of my call.
I push in her number. Of course, she is sleeping,
but after a few rings she answers.

And we talk for a while about all the places
we want to travel to and where we want to settle down.
And she says that she should really get back to sleep,
and so should I, which I agree to.

Goodbye, I will talk to you tomorrow night.

In a night that shows my breath
I start walking back up the hill to my own bed,
so I can go to sleep too.

Shannon Hughes

Kite

She stretches him across over the wooden frame. His tense bare back is a cloth of knots, she pulls them apart, each tangled thread, putting a few large pink marbles of muscle in her mouth to dissolve them like sugar cubes. She folds his sharp edges over to make smooth perfect creases. From his eyelashes she begins to braid a tail. She takes from his bottom lip one golden strand for a string to pilot his diamond-shaped form. She carries him under her arm to a wide green field and waits for wind.

Alexis Kielb

Fingerprints

he ended up coming to dinner.

it wasn't exactly as I had planned,
he sat at my table
dipping an artichoke heart
into melted butter
which dripped
down the five o'clock shadow
of his chin.

later that night
I found fingerprints,
elliptical and smeared,
inching toward my place
and retreating.

Caroline Hagood

Cold

It was a window of a conversation because they both leaned out of it
Speaking in euphemisms and baring their faces to the cold
As their bodies remained heated, stretched close to the window
As the window remained warmed by their voices

It was a sweet pair of talkers with their eyes facing the avenue of sight
And their hands close but not grazing each other
It seemed that the lust was impossible; at the moment she felt it,
She was removed by wind, saying: if only it were lust that carried me away

It was a sad conversation which was embittered by their different aims
She wanted fresh air and he wanted her
And wasn't it refreshing to be wanted?
Always, but she thought it would be more refreshing to want

Sharon Zetter

NC17

That first time, when I was young
and wishing that I was beautiful, I let him
put his hands up my shirt. We were alone
in the balcony, except
for his best friend in the first row.
I felt the sticky floor through my sandals
as he stroked my breasts,
telling me they were perfect
and beautiful and I tried to believe
him. I really did. But I knew

better, because in the semi-darkness
of the theatre he couldn't see
their freckles or the stretch marks.
And as Demi Moore stripped
for the camera, I felt
his hands
on my jeans, on the zipper.
And he was begging, begging me.

Please?

And I closed my eyes, the dirt collecting
on my eyelids as he attempted
to fuck me in his clumsy,
teenage boy way.

I played the role, moaning
at all the right times. I became Slut,
as I pretended
I didn't notice his best friend still sitting
in the front row,
watching.

Rebecca Ciralsky

The Octopus

"A tame ride," my boyfriend
says once the man
with the cigarette butt hanging
from his cracked lips latches us
into the paint-torn compartment.
And then the spinning, twirling ellipses that
hadn't looked so horrible
when I had seen them from the ticket counter.
Already the nausea licks
at the back of my throat, way deep
down, the birthday cake
from the barbecue I had just tasted an hour
earlier. My neck goes limp, hardly able to breathe
Lamaze-like—breath two, breath three, my whole body
convulsing like the dead
woman dancing with Tom Petty in his video
"Last Dance with Mary Jane." His voice whispers
softly into my ear, "Do you know how beautiful
you look right now," in that sick
shade of green, my mouth parting slightly
to exhale. "We are going to make it next
year, you and I...you know how much I love
you?" But all I remember is the last
time when the guy puked off the Flipper
and it landed splat onto the corrugated
metal like coins falling from a pocket.

Jennifer Bonhomme

For Dan

He was confused.
Callus-fingered, nostrils ripe red

He asked me why I was crying.
I told him because I fucking felt like it.

That I was drunk
and that's what I do when I am drunk.

Before his mouth grazed my body,
we talked.

He told me stories
of how he stole cell phones from cars for cocaine.

"It was like an adventure mission,"
he slurred and I squinted at him through haze.

I felt the gin replace my blood,
pumping through every part of my body.

It was warm and sour.
I wonder if he tasted it.

I think I was smoking
but that was after we talked.

The cigarettes were perched on the table
next to the ceramic lamp shaped like a Spanish dancer.

The party had died down except for a few hot bodies.
Erica and Dave were fucking in the bed,

while Sarah sat in the corner, watching Letterman,
laughing too loud.

And I sat in a chair
with a washcloth covering my bare chest
staring at him,

Begging him to hold me
on top of the plastic sheets.

Amara Dante Verona

After She Was a Girl

The boy's hands move up her back
under her shirt, perhaps blindly, or maybe looking
for something she has and will abandon to him   or something she has
but will keep from him   or something she doesn't have at all.
She can't feel his skin, only the cold of his fingers
that make her skin tighten painfully, nipples harden,
as the freeze spreads.

There are so many questions to ask at times like these
but they should never be: *Why are you crying?*
And *What's wrong?* (Feminine words clumsy in a boy's mouth.)
He should have been quiet
or simply used his fingertips
to wipe the wet over her face so it wouldn't drip

But he expected an answer, and so she answered,
desperate, or horrified, or resigned: (looking into the bonfire, thinking
of the flammable woods, choking on the desperateness of it all)
They've made me into a girl. Relieved,
(she is only being irrational) he says: *You've always been a girl.*

Sasha Haines-Stiles

Summer Crush

We sat together for a month
before I asked him if he'd consider
being more like me.
I wondered aloud
why he liked the way I wore my hair:
no one else did.
We held hands,
he had the courage to kiss my neck
like a vampire
and I just couldn't bring myself to tell him
it was fall.

Samara Adsit Holtz

Circuitry

1
The dress made of poppies—
I slide my hands between the petals.
Laid out on my bed it's a landscape
set on fire. It will pour red
over me as though it owns me.

2
White. Spark, sugar.
This March the sky glows white on us,
closing our eyes. Silent. I can feel the
season. You make me
think of air, of pale oxygen.

3
You try to think of all things
that are yellow. Light amber. Lemons.
One bowl in your house. One shirt. A white
flower with a tiny yellow center.
In your dream last night, you walked
into an empty room with
me and I said your name three times;
the walls were hard yellow.

4
At 2:40 p.m. I am listening to
your voice from the other end of town.
I hold the telephone with both
hands. It's bright blue, like a strobe light.
I can hear your sounds turn
the color of water as they come to
me. The telephone cord is a vein.

5
I pretend the carpet is a pond.
Stepping into its muscular green, I drop
onto my back, trying to float with my
arms stretched open, the ceiling
like new leaves. I wear a red dress that
drags on the nap of the carpet. My
skin reflects green as heat collects between
the floor and my spine.

Samara Adsit Holtz

Our Mercurial Bodies Make Their Own Grief

1

Fed by the blazing
summer season, I've kept house in myself,
living on like coals left after
a watch fire.

In the margin of a book, in tiny letters
almost crushing each other, I write
about your body: *his hands are narrower*
than mine. The skin over his ribs is
paraffin.

2

Bloodthirst, bloodheat, bloodbitter.
Blood is magnetic, radioactive, quick
as a fuse.
First, second, third chance. To cry
tears of blood. To feel my heart open,
clutch, the blood cleaving
to its own self.

3

We constantly shed our skins;

your surface thins to the point of
transparence, and I witness your melding bones
and tendons.
Your shadow pooling like mica.

When I cross your body, from one side
to the other, it's like trading a life on
one coast for life on its opposite.

4

Come evening—band of shade, a lodestar—
fluttering electric light wings batter
the air of my bedroom, spreading from an
exposed bulb. Below,
my shoulder blades form a close bundle.
In my mind, I go through words
for you: nascent beloved, sleeper, fickle
skin, a mark washed off.

My sleeping body walks the heat-scarred
fields. The wind gulping with its juiceless
tongue. Grasses hooked together
like vertebrae.

Sasha Haines-Stiles

Rib

You're the only man who knows
what it's like to give birth.
I was born of a piece of you,
snug under your skin until
you needed a wife
to help you keep the garden clean.
Would you rather I had stayed
where a rib's supposed to stay?
I would have grown within you
like a cancer grows—
like a rib repairing itself,
I would have knit myself together:
eyes clear like wedges of perfect blue sky
hair like the lush vines you cut down,
breasts like fruits,
like the apple I ate
that you hate me for eating.
Would you leave me?
Do you need me now?
A rib's such a tiny bone.
But I am your baby,
life that swelled up within you,
bursting out only to love you more,
with every breath living to please you.
Adam, you are my mother.
How can it be otherwise—
how could you not love your child?

Julia Cohen

The Spoon

Even before I met you, I wanted
to feed your hunger until it dissolved
in a sigh. A stale cigarette can still start
a forest fire. Your pockets brimmed
with matches.

I cradled your fears in a spoon,
the venom evaporating with the heat.
I never let your tongue burn.

When I sipped from your well of thought,
I scraped dry caverns, jutting rocks,
and desperate caves. There is nothing I want less
than your acidic aftertaste.

Zoe Konovalov

Marrow

All you've got is a bowl of blackberries like blood
and you slurp on it. Your red tongue arcs like a wire
to lick your red chin and you grin at me,
raise black black eyebrows.
You grin at me across the table,
over your plate of carcasses,
crunching marrow, sucking gristle, loving the fat on your chin,
eating my heart, cracking hollow bones and
hurling clammy
chunks for the dogs.

Your breath sounds like a slaughterhouse
when you slam me against the wall and bite my tongue.
I think I'd like to be crucified, or burnt at the stake.
Either way I'd like to be consumed, don't let
my blood fall onto dust, don't let it spill into rivers,
please, suck it all up.

I hoped I'd left you behind
although the fumes still followed me
and I smelled you on my skin.
And I'll remember you whenever I light a match
and wake the yellow sulfur
and I'll remember the last time you kissed me—
you know, the bushfire of dried sticks,
your jagged teeth, your black black mouth, your tender hungry eyes—
a long kiss, and worth exactly nothing.

Karen Emmerich

Leave-taking

there is the creak
of bedsprings
as you rise to the glare
of early-morning
darkness, that nervous
anticipation of light

you leave
the windows open,
now all I can hear
is curtains—the snap
of wind on fabric,
of fabric compressing air

I picture my breath
solid and white,
unfurling
like a canvas sail to catch
that stinging wind—

hallelujah
I am forsaken

Annie Lee

Letter to a Ghetto Boy Three Thousand Miles Away

I tried to forget you, boy
softsweet
who sat beside me on the preschool bus, giving me the head of your
      rooster costume on
Halloween, older, massaging my foot as I cried in rhythm to the
      muggings on the street,
soothing me with your love of Monty Python, your desire to
      write plays
except you weren't smart enough and wrote too small,
      who smuggled butterscotches
from the lame candy vendor—here, here, here—
      and hollowed eggs by blowing yolk
onto the street, hoping to hit angry pedestrians, then
      painting the shells with Chinese characters.
Sitting beside me on the fire escape, telling me I was a star
      that would one day disappear from here

I tried to forget

your faint Tahiti accent tripping through my ear like fingers pressing upon
the spine, the murmuring of your waltzing joints as you walked, the shysmile
that peeked out from your hoodlum mask of false confidence,
your personality that transcended clothing and
neighborhood. How you cursed and recited Bible stories at night when my
      father was
drunk, and showed me how to do laundry and iron shirts I tried to
      forget. Forget.

But you lingered
like a kiss

like that

in my thoughts: I could see you in my nails, the curve of my eyebrows, my
      urine and body hair
lingered until I wanted to melt into your skin, kissing by the four-inch
scar on the upper right arm, the pin-drop mole an elbow away, to nestle
inside your pinky, pinky that swayed in motion to Schubert.

You lingered,
love of my innocence, even after I left, flew away like you said and tried
      to forget.

Elizabeth Bear

Confessions from Gilcrease

Sitting on the steps of the museum porch,
an odd chill in the air for a July afternoon.
You had such guitarist fingers, holding Marlboros all the time
or resting them on your coffee mug and in your pockets.
I thought they'd fly off your outstretched arms
to write music on the wall.
So while I ate my sandwich and told you my poems
and wondered if anyone would smell your smoke in my hair
you told me how you lay on your floor for three days,
turning your head and looking past my eyes as though the contact,
though not physical, would be uncontrollable
your ponytail falling down,
the stubble on your chin not manly, just lazy.
Nothing but ceiling and spider webs for seventy-two hours.
How many cigarettes and visions?
Were you reduced to counting footsteps overhead
and water drips into the rusted sink?
Your days spent falling asleep,
getting up to piss, giving the refrigerator a weary stare;
food was far from your mind.
You never thought it was stupid to go away
with the purpose of lying in your dirty apartment,
there was nothing strange about trying to get your priorities straight.
You said it was a depression
that made you disappear into the stained carpet.
You said it was the way the world pressed into your skin,
the way too many decisions render you impotent,
but then it could have been any depression or moment.
You could have said anything to me, the day was a dream.
Even the important things were forgotten;
only the idea of a confession remains.
The space between us was too frightening to cross alone,
a few feet, a few years.
How long will we regret that?

Jeffrey Chiu

Three Notes on a Kitchen Table

Slipped on some ice yesterday morning, stumbled over the heavy garbage cans, tipped them over. Stared at the mess of chicken bones, cereal boxes, crumpled tissues. Went back inside. Slept uncomfortably all day. Didn't answer the phone. Noticed the branches outside gently blending into the evening sky while boiling noodles for supper. Ate in silence. Thought about you, the length of time over which our correspondence has lasted. Have withheld nothing so far in the letters, gave you even the weather: how overcast, the humidity, the number of degrees below zero. Peeked out the door near midnight to see furry scavengers rummaging through the discarded leftovers, scattering them across the lawn.

* * *

Mailed another letter to you today. Sat on a bench in the park, with the intention of relaxing. Enjoyed the tranquility. Saw an old lady, the postman, a shadowy neighbor walk by. Felt terrible. Stayed in the park until the children started to arrive. Considered walking over to the playground swings, but decided I wasn't one to judge myself deserving. Was approached by a homeless man. Shook my head slowly until he walked away, disappeared.

* * *

Thanked the mailman, placed your letter aside for tonight. Remembered the letter you sent weeks ago, whose page with the word "self-centered" I read twelve times. Convinced myself I fully understood it after two days. Can't remember what it said right this minute, though. Am expected at work in half an hour. Feel desperately retarded now as I recall how you wrote, as though a sage, "There are punishments and rewards." Adapting fine, I inwardly assure. I'm finishing this note to you, to nobody. I'm leaving this table. Here I am at near completion. I'm anxious for your words. You're really just a habit.

Ryan Hagan

Serendipity, I thought

Serendipity, I thought
They're playing our song
and I folded against
a shelf of cranberries.

Summer supermarket air;
a child has jammed the automatic doors
open with leeks.

My only one
puffy-eyed girl
tiny red canvas shoes.

You are ensconced in the papaya.
You are cross-legged in the honeydew.
You are curled in the red cabbage.

But you are none of these places
and the lobsters, claws tied shut,
struggle awkwardly, inaudibly, in their tank.

But you are miles distant
and Epictetus, deriding stock boy,
sits smugly behind the smug meat counter.

And I had thought: serendipity
but you are none of these places
and produce is never nepenthe enough.

Michael Casper

Picayunes

casually thinking of you & new york city,
orange and oranges and picayunes
and you and
casually thinking of
bathtubs: that one in the smokysmall
upstairs, garnished red wallpaper
in wintertime fresh smells and such
to touch tension and tension
and the palm of my hand

you and small change you
holding my ended and broken
stretches cynical in excess
except evenings when worthlessnesses
"what are you afraid of"-says.

                  this and more
but look, our akimbos are matching
and you are fogged and uppity at dawn
peeling fruit and mocking my smile.
i'm contentedly offended
                     by everything you say

Grace Lorentz

Youthful Gods Flirting

At midnight I wake from a nightmare. My eyes are luminous spots of white staring at the ceiling. I take a long breath, and with a shaky hand I push my damp hair off my forehead.

At midnight I am taking a cool shower. My pajamas are in a lonely heap on the pale tile floor. I run my fingers through my hair and the water flows over my closed eyes and lips.

At midnight I dress and turn off the bathroom light. The stairs are silky under my water-softened feet.

In the living room I go to the piano and sit in a rolling chair in front of it. There is no light except that of the moon. A fishbowl has been left in an open window, and swaying leaves and the moonlight make patterns in it. I imagine walking on the smooth, seaweed-covered pebbles with the light flickering around me. The fish sleeps.

At midnight I play Beethoven's *Moonlight Sonata*. The pages of the music are illuminated by the clear, white light of the moon. My hands are ghosts, dancing alone, over the keys. My arms are hidden in shadow.

Outside there is a deep grumbling in the sky, and I look toward the open window. Black clouds race to steal the moon's seat in the heavens. The fishbowl is dark, and I move it out of the window. Its owner wakes and swims in a slow circle. I lean out the window and look into the sky, expectantly.

With a flash of lightning I see him, high up in the tree. His cheek rests on an inky branch and he smiles at me. His lips are glowing purple.

The thunder rattles the house and I return his smile. He leaps from the tree, black against a deep grape sky and lands outside the window. His bare feet curl in the wet grass. I lean to him and help him climb inside, dripping on the dry, dusty floor.

At midnight there is a band in the living room. A saxophone screams and the fingers of an ancient man slam and jump over ivory keys. A trumpet player curves backwards and sings in his horn's voice. Crazy rain does the drumming on the walls.

Our hearts keep time in our chests and we dance. We twirl and dip and sweat and breathe until our bodies are tired and mutter like old trees. Slowly the rain runs out. The band fades away.

I bid him go then, as he stretches in a blue doorway.

"I hear the moon crying."

"Time is dying in his cell."

For a moment he is still. I look down at my bare feet on the floor and yawn. He smiles and leaps backward out the window, kicking a midnight rainbow across the sky.

At midnight I put the fishbowl back into the window and walk quietly to the stairs. The moonlight flickers on the banister. Again the fish sleeps. I slide my hand on the wooden railing as I climb up.

A bit after midnight, I close my eyes in bed.

Erica Magrey

The First Time

the first time,
i closed my eyes when i thought you knew
and leaned forward
dipped into
some lush creamsicle
i dreamed about at age five

it was always
the bells
a truck turning the corner, sounding like
the fourth of july
the explosion
of taste buds
in bittersweet exchange

Deborah Stein

Unearned Chance

Last night I dreamt you came back
throwing rocks at my window
beating your breast in an artificial fog
serenading on a banjo
you began again
romantic again
you who said I made you a cynic
waving that eager adolescent letter
like a scroll
written on rose petals
making me remember
spelling mistakes and tear stains
now a new performance
and as the fog machines whirred
and the spotlight clicked on
I leaned over my balcony
and said yes.

Elizabeth Hazen

Laundry Day

You had method
more meticulous than a maid
as you washed: let the clothes
soak five minutes, then wring them
dry and rinse twice.

In the shady place
on the stone steps beneath
the lemon trees you sat,
happy to have cold water up
to your elbows,

happy to have an afternoon
like this to do wash
and nothing else, happy
to have me watching over you
like a mother or a sister

and no more. Just a silent
finger pointing out soap bubbles
and specks of dirt. A small voice
filling the lucid air
with color.

I wanted to throw water
or sunlight, but I did not move or speak
louder than a whisper;
I did not want to disturb
the wisps of hair in your eyes.

I will never forget
that green washbasin
or the way the wind blew the box of detergent
into the garden, or the way,
when I helped you wring out

the wet clothes and our skin touched,
it was no more than wet skin
against wet skin. That touching of our damp,
expectant fingers in soapy water
was enough.

Nadja Blagojevic

Expert

I am an expert
on the way your hair curls
when we're both dripping salt
and waves are breaking
over the bow of the ship.

I am well acquainted
with the bones in your back,
your narrow hips,
your lonely ribs.

I know which hollow of your chest
most perfectly resounds
the pounding of that furious muscle.

I know the width of your arms
the breadth of your shoulders
the inflections of your voice
and the inferences of your expressive eyes,
and you are still cabalistic, complex.

With our arms at funny angles,
our hands make love,
calluses
nails
cuticles
tendons and
small bones.

Annie Lee

Wrist

Your wrist speaks to me
A dancing wrist
Whirling,
Beckoning, and chanting
Weaving a tale
of fragile sensuality

The wrist of your lips
Smashing
through heavy air,
Of your legs and thighs,
Peeling it like orange skin

I love the wrist of your eyes, how it bends
A seduction
And I can smell the scent in your hair
Hear the song of the wrist and its whispers
Promises
of champagne and Chopin
Your wrist that lingers
like cigarette smoke, slowly
curling
to sleep at the nape of my neck

Jaime Halla

Ginger Ale

Dozing in the corner
of your love seat
my head on the wooden
armrest and my legs
spread over your lap
I can smell the detergent
in the blankets
and the stale heat
sliding down my forehead

I wonder if you'll still
taste like ginger ale
and peppermints when
you're forty and I'm
thirty-four, and whether
I'll be with you to find out.

Julia Schaffer

Driving Miss Daisy (PG 13)

We were on a date and I'd never been on one before.
We walked to the movie theater, our bladders tender
With the water and Coke we had gulped to be in time

For *Driving Miss Daisy*. We swung our arms as we walked
The air pricked between us. We were like enemies almost
And when you asked for two tickets and they turned you

Away, my mouth snapped for blame. I bit on my lip
Not knowing romance, knowing only fretful petting.
What a tame movie. We wore sneakers, how could they

Fear us and bar us from the theater? Should we part ways?
Go home and mope? We had exhausted the limits of sociability
Over lunch. Of all the movies. Of all the days. Didn't we look

Thirteen, my breasts? My braces, yes, were a drawback.
What was there to hide from us two New York kids, slick and sour
So accustomed to avoiding others' eyes we couldn't see each other.

What could Jessica Tandy have that we hadn't busted open
And got bored with months ago? So tears singed my eyes.
I smelled a vendor's incense and it stung. I prayed you wouldn't

Comfort me as tears struck my cheeks and the wind froze them.
Damn you, making me cry. Don't look. Don't touch me. And then
You too, frustrated, weary from a night of boosting yourself up for

Some quintessential moment, cried. We turned away. With my fists
I wiped off tears and walked so briskly I had to stop and wait at the corner,
I couldn't calm myself till you caught up and said, "Those idiots."

"Yeah. They were." We walked, with every word moving closer, till
Our elbows hit. "Those idiots." We walked down the block to the other
movie theater. We knew they'd let us in to see *Joe Versus the Volcano*.

Drew Krewer

The Zipper

It was the night of the sixth grade dance,
and I opened the door to my closet,
and there, four pairs in a row,
were jeans I had outgrown. I wanted to pass time,
to feel fabric crush my knobbed knees, my thin calves.
So I pulled them out, flung each pair on the carpet.
I tried to enter one pair, my foot too big to pass through
the blue denim tunnel. Then another pair, another.
And I thrust my foot, reached the end of a hollow leg,
the material tight against my middle school thighs;
it was like I was backtracking years of my life,
going past my fifth birthday, my first ride at the county fair,
my first word. With my bare back pressed hard
against the dirty bedroom carpet, I began to zip.
The zipper climbed slowly, tooth by tooth; it trembled
with accomplishment. It ran against my penis,
my glans swelling and throbbing.
And when the zipper reached the top,
it felt as if all the blood and nerve of my body
had pooled in my crotch, as if god was trapped in my testicles
and finally found his way out. I quickly unzipped the jeans,
pulled them down to my jutting ankles, pulled down my underwear,
and the semen glistened—opaque like sweet milk.

My body was a constant mystery, then;
penis and vagina were only two lonely body parts,
and sex was just another thing my grandmother worried about,
like a severe thunderstorm warning
or not having fresh bread at the end of the week.

And later that night, when the disco ball shined,
when the multicolored Christmas lights flashed,
when the girls and boys danced
arm-lengths apart, I found myself going back to my room,
zipping, zipping, zipping,
relishing that moment when the cells surged
from my body, slicked my skin, and told me
where I had come from, where I could go.

Notes on Contributors

Please note: This information about contributors was current as *Shooting the Rat* was going to press in the spring of 2003.

Nafeesah Allen
Milton Academy, Milton, Massachusetts, 2002
Nafeesah Allen graduated from Milton Academy in June, 2002 with the Leo Maza Cultural Award. She worked as a program intern in a municipal Division of Employment and Training. She plans to participate in a five year International Studies Program (bachelor's and master's degrees) with a minor in journalism. She is also in the process of creating a magazine that will serve her hometown area, Newark, New Jersey.

Rebecca Alston-Milkman
Hunter College High School, New York City, 1994.
Rebecca Alston-Milkman graduated Phi Beta Kappa in 1998 from Wesleyan University with a double major in dance and sociology, and high honors in dance. Since then she has co-founded the dance company Good Milkman with Rebecca Good, and her choreography has been shown in several New York City venues, including the Evolving Arts Theater, University Settlement and Access Theater. In April of 2002, she moved to the Los Angeles area.

Mia Alvar
Marymount School, New York City, 1996
Mia Alvar was born in the Philippines and attended high school in New York City. She was editor-in-chief of her high school literary magazine, *The Muse*, and a co-representative of her class.

Ian Kain Amato
Nassau BOCES Cultural Arts Center, Syosset, New York, 2001
Since participating in the Provincetown Shadow Writing Project, Ian Kain Amato has taught two creative writing groups for teens. He is presently teaching writing to high school students in the One Voice Writing Project at the Garden City Public Library. He is pursuing an associate's degree at Nassau Community College, after which he plans to join the Peace Corps and work in Asia.

Katina Zoe Antoniades
Brighton High School. Rochester, New York, 1997
Katina Zoe Antoniades attended Bryn Mawr College and majored in English with a concentration in creative writing and a minor in anthropology. During the fall semester of her junior year, she studied at King's College London. She recently earned her master's degree in magazine, newspaper, and online journalism from the S. I. Newhouse School of Public Communications at Syracuse University. As we went to press, she was working part time in Rochester, NY, and looking for a job in journalism, publishing, or public relations.

Lauren Argintar
Blake High School of the Arts, Tampa, Florida, 2001.

Erin Beach Himelright
North Kitsap High School, Poulsbo, Washington, 2000
Erin Beach Himelright graduated from Edmonds Community College in Lynnwood, Washington, in June, 2001 with an associate's degree. She was married in February, 2001 and presently lives with her husband in Chico, California. As we went to press, they were expecting their first child.

Elizabeth Bear
Owasso High School, Owasso Oklahoma, 2001
Elizabeth Bear attended the National Book Foundation's summer writing camp as a high school student. Her poems have appeared in *Teenlink* and McGregor Publishing's High School Anthology.

Nadja Blagojevic
Orono High School, Orono, Maine, 2002
After graduation from Orono High, Nadja Blagojevic is spending a fifth year of high school in Germany. Having spent a month in an intensive language course in the countryside of old East Germany, she will be moving to the most densely populated region of Germany, near the Dutch border. Though her acquaintance with the German language began only recently, she hopes to complete the year with a level of fluency high enough to allow her to read Rilke and Goethe in the original. She plans to enter Stanford University in the fall of 2003, and hopes to study some combination of linguistics, philosophy and psychology while continuing to write poetry and prose.

Jennifer Bonhomme
Tenafly High School, Tenafly, New Jersey, 2001
Jennifer Bonhomme attended New Jersey's Governor's School for the Arts in the summer between her junior and senior years of high school.

Lauren Brozovich
University School of Milwaukee, Milwaukee, Wisconsin, 1996
Lauren Brozovich won the Thomas T. Hoopes Prize for outstanding scholarly work at Harvard, where she graduated in 2001 with a BA in English. She was also awarded a Mellon Fellowship in Humanistic Studies by the Woodrow Wilson National Fellowship Foundation to pursue doctoral study in English literature.

Jessica Bulman
Amherst Regional High School, Amherst, Massachusetts, 1998
Jessica Bulman graduated *summa cum laude* from Yale University in May 2002. She received the Chauncey Brewster Tinker Prize for the outstanding senior English major at Yale, as well as the Norton Scholar's Prize for the best literary essay by an undergraduate in the United States. She is currently a Gates Scholar at Cambridge University, England, where she is pursuing an MPhil in English literature.

Emily Carmichael
Stuyvesant High School, New York City, 2000
Emily Carmichael attends Harvard University, where she finally decided to study painting and literature. The second flashiest thing she ever did was win the Bertelsmann Award for Fiction and Literature when she was a high school senior. The third was probably the effort to promote a play she had written by putting on a ball gown and having a tea party with a teddy bear outside the student union.

Michael Casper
Cambridge School of Weston, Weston, Massachusetts, 2002
Michael Casper graduated from the Cambridge School of Weston in June of 2002 and now attends Reed College in Portland, Oregon.

Jeffery Chiu
Stuyvesant High School, New York City, 1994
After graduating in 1998 *magna cum laude* and Phi Beta Kappa from the State University of New York at Buffalo, where he was an English major, Jeffery Chiu went on to graduate study at the University of Washington in Seattle. His list of current, tentative and potential interests includes literary theory and criticism, Asian American history and literature, 20th Century American literature, post-structuralism, cultural studies, various discourses on race and ethnicity, the culture(s) of technology, and sexuality. He adds that his list "seems to change every few months."

Rebecca Ciralsky Levin
University School of Milwaukee, Milwaukee, Wisconsin, 1977
Rebecca Ciralsky Levin graduated from the University of Virginia in May 2001, where she majored in Spanish and minored in Italian. She was Phi Beta Kappa and a member of the Golden Key Honor Society. Recently married, she lives with her husband in Richmond, Virginia, where she works for an insurance broker/consultant. She is in the process of applying to law school for fall 2003.

Philip Clark
Yorktown High School, 1998
Philip Clark has published a number of poems, essays, and reviews since his appearance in *Hanging Loose*. His magazine and journal credits include *Lambda Book Report*, *The James White Review*, and *UnderStudy*. Recently, he has written and published articles surrounding his main research interest, the Victorian-era photographer F. Holland Day. He graduated Phi Beta Kappa from the College of William and Mary in May, 2002.

Jesse Cohen
Jesse Cohen is a senior at Saint Ann's School in Brooklyn. She writes that she "lives with her two wonderful parents and an enormous cat in Manhattan. A curious and contemplative young woman, she is an explorer of realms both physical and mental, and loves to document her travels in any and every way that she can."

Julia Cohen
Concord Academy, Concord, Massachusetts, 2000
Julia Cohen, a junior English major at Wesleyan, has had a number of poems and short stories published in a variety of literary journals. She spent a semester in England, taking creative writing classes, and has worked as an editorial intern for the New York University Press.

Gemma Cooper-Novack
Saint Ann's School, Brooklyn, New York, 2000
Gemma Cooper-Novack is a junior at the University of Chicago, concentrating in linguistics and anthropology. Her poetry has appeared in *Euphony, ByLine*, and the chapbook *Saint Ann's at Saint Mark's*. Her articles have appeared in the *University of Chicago Free Press*. She is a theater director and a puppeteer, and she teaches theater and puppetry to children.

Susan Currie
Incarnate Word High School, La Vernia, Texas, 1996
Susan Currie was a founder of the Texas Young Writers' Association and served as its president and newsletter editor.

Lucy Cutolo
Brooklyn Poly Prep, Brooklyn, New York, 1996
Lucy Cutolo tells us she liked Courtney Love a lot better than she liked high school.

Jesse Dalbacka
Perpich Center for Arts Education, Golden Valley, Minnesota, 2000
Jesse Dalbacka is presently at the University of Minnesota, Twin Cities, working on a major in American Studies and a minor in Chinese. These areas of interest do coalesce: Through the University, she has twice had the opportunity to live and travel in China. She has studied everything from the language to city structures to Beijing opera, but her newest area of obsession is the history, complexity, significance, and possible future of American popular culture in China. She is still writing, but she has given up cooking jobs in the interests of school and sleep. Instead, she works for the Minnesota Orchestra.

Ian Demsky
Eastern Michigan University, Detroit, Michigan, 1996
Ian Demsky completed his senior year of high school at Eastern Michigan University through a dual enrollment program. His work has appeared in *The Santa Barbara Review, Pen & Ink Magazine*, and *Sulfur*.

Caitlin Doyle
Miss Porter's School, Farmington, Connecticut, 2000
Caitlin Doyle is currently studying at the University of North Carolina, Chapel Hill. She is the first recipient of that university's Thomas Wolfe Scholarship—a full four-year creative writing scholarship, which includes summer travel and study. She is majoring in English, with a minor in creative writing.

Erica Ehrenberg
Hunter College High School, New York City 1996
Erica Ehrenberg grew up in New York City, where she attended Hunter College High School and studied poetry with Kip Zegers. She was an English/creative writing major at Amherst College where she worked with Glyn Maxwell and wrote as her thesis a collection of poems, *Films of the Ocean Floor*. She currently lives in Brooklyn and attends New York University's Creative Writing Program.

Karen Emmerich
Ward Melville High School, East Setauket, New York, 1996
Karen Emmerich earned her BA from Princeton University in 2000, with a major in comparative literature and certificates in Hellenic studies and creative writing. She earned her MA in comparative literature from the University of Thessaloniki in 2002, and is currently pursuing a PhD in English and comparative literature at Columbia University. She is the recipient of Fulbright, Onassis, and Mellon fellowships, as well as the Elizabeth Constantinides Translation Prize. She is the translator of *The Few Things I Know About Glafkos Thrassakis*, by Vassilis Vassilikos (Seven Stories Press, 2002).

Rebecca Givens
Chamblee High School, Atlanta, Georgia, 1999
Rebecca Givens is an English major at Yale, class of 2003. Her poems are published or upcoming in *The Georgia Review, The Gettysburg Review, The Cortland Review, Poet Lore* and others. She was a national finalist for the Ruth Lilly Fellowship and has won Yale's Bergen, Meeker, Veach, and Willets poetry, fiction, and composition prizes. She attended a summer research symposium in cognitive science at the University of Pennsylvania, studied philosophy at the University of Heidelberg, and undertook a Kilbourne Memorial Travel Fellowship for senior essay research in Oxford and London. Her interests include poetics and the philosophy of mind.

Alexis Love Goldberg
Saint Ann's School, Brooklyn, New York, 2000
Alexis Goldberg is currently a junior at Northwestern University where she is majoring in English and performance studies. At college she combines her love of writing and theater with collaborative pieces involving poetry and performance. She was involved in an original student production based on text and movement which she both wrote and performed; she also wrote and performed a spoken word piece as a prelude to a production of *The Dutchman*. She spent one summer working as a teacher's aide at the East River Child Development Center, a school for disabled young children. She hopes to continue to combine her writing with other pursuits in the coming years.

Marianna Green
Robert Louis Stevenson High School, Pebble Beach, California, 1996
After graduating high school, Marianna Green attended the University of California at Berkeley.

Dan Gruenberg
The Hotchkiss School, Lakeville, Connecticut, 1997
Dan Gruenberg graduated from Harvard College in 2002 with a concentration in history. He writes that the girl in this poem had serious personal difficulty "at an age when she was not equipped to deal with such a problem. Now...she has a successful career in a profession she cares about...I wrote this because I was angry that life was unfair to her, but impressed at her defiant ability to confront the world."

Ryan Hagan
Wauwatosa East High School, Wauwatosa, Wisconsin, 2001
Ryan Hagan is studying English and creative writing at New York University.

Caroline Hagood
Saint Ann's School, Brooklyn, New York, 2000
Caroline Hagood is a junior at Vassar College, majoring in English. She spent a semester abroad in Madrid. She continues to write poetry in her free time.

Sasha Haines-Stiles
Pingry School, Martinsville, New Jersey, 1998

Jaime Halla
Wheeling High School, Wheeling, Illinois, 1995
Jaime Halla went on after high school to study at Northeast Missouri State University.

Olivia Ophelia Harman
Princeton Day School, Princeton, New Jersey, 2000
Olivia Harman studies philosophy, psychology, and writing at Swarthmore College. In 2003 she spent a semester abroad at the University of East Anglia, where she was hoping to write plays and sing backup in British bands.

Elizabeth Hazen
Walt Whitman High School, Potomac Maryland, 1997

Beth Herskovits
Stuyvesant High School, New York City, 1999
Beth Herskovits is a senior English major at Cornell University where she serves as editor-in-chief of *The Cornell Daily Sun*. In 1999, she won first place, citywide, in the Bertelsmann's World of Expression Scholarship Competition in the category of fiction. She is planning to pursue a career in journalism after graduation.

Samara Adsit Holtz
Home Schooled, Greensboro, Vermont, 2002
Samara Adsit Holtz was a member of an adult writers' group while being home schooled and published work in *Poetry in Motion*, *The*

Parnassus Literary Journal, and *Grab-A-Nickel*. The last we heard from her, she was working in a nursing home in Vermont, contemplating college, and writing poems. Her work has recently appeared in the regular pages of *Hanging Loose*.

Erin Hoover
Cumberland Valley High School, Mechanicsburg, Pennsylvania, 1997
Erin Hoover studied creative writing (among other things) at Sarah Lawrence College, where she was awarded the Sarah Lawrence Review poetry prize. She continues to write and she lives and works in New York. Her work has appeared in *The Harrisburg Review, California Quarterly, Tarnhelm, The Sarah Lawrence Review,* and *The Bard Papers*.

Shannon Hughes
Saint Ann's School, Brooklyn, New York, 1995
After high school Shannon Hughes majored in political science at Barnard College. While there she participated in the pilot year of a mentoring program in writing for teenage girls and, following her 1999 graduation, helped develop the program, named Girls Write Now (currently seeking non-profit status and funding, and celebrating its fifth year). She is also pursuing her master's degree in social work at New York University. She hopes to continue working with adolescents and the arts.

Julia Jarcho
Hunter College High School, New York City, 1999
Julia Jarcho's first play, *Nursery*, was produced at the Cherry Lane Alternative as part of the 2001 Young Playwrights Festival. She has since developed work as a writer-in-residence at the Eugene O'Neill Playwrights Conference (2002) and in production at Harvard College, where she studies literature. She recently received a 2002 Berilla Kerr Award for playwriting. As a performer, she has appeared in new stage pieces by Richard Maxwell, Jim Strahs, Aaron Landsman, and Tory Vazquez. Her poems have been published in the *Harvard Advocate* and *American Poet*.

Jenny Jones
Balfron High School, Glasgow, Scotland, 2002
Jenny Jones is currently living in China, teaching English on a gap year between leaving high school and starting university studies. When she returns to Scotland, she plans to study either medicine or history and politics, but intends to keep writing. She recently won an award in the national Young Writers Competition in Scotland; she worked in her school to publish a creative writing magazine entitled *Freedom of Speech* which was well received by local and national authorities and was sold to benefit Amnesty International.

Mathew Joy
Loyola High School, Pasadena, California, 1999
Matthew Joy is in his fourth and final year at Columbia University, where he's majoring in English and Spanish. While at Columbia he studied writ-

ing with the late Kenneth Koch. He also studied in Scotland. He hopes to go to law school back on the west coast in 2004.

Amy Kenna
Sehome High School, Bellingham, Washington, 1999
Amy Kenna attended Carleton College in Northfield, Minnesota, where she was the two-time winner of the Huntington Poetry Prize and editor-in-chief of the *Carletonian*. She majored in political science and studio art. She is currently a reporter at the *Shelby Daily Star* in Shelby, North Carolina.

Keystone (Robert Elstein)
Edward R. Murrow High School, Brooklyn, New York, 1996
Robert Elstein studied literature and drama at Sarah Lawrence College. Since graduation, he has been working 9 to 5 in the publishing industry and studying poetry with Larry Fagin. He has had poems published in *The Sarah Lawrence Review, Sal Mimeo,* and *Insurance.* He now writes under his birth name and lives in Park Slope, Brooklyn. About his poem in this collection, "Fida Fida Fida Fida," he says it's "a poem about the modest surprises of everyday living, and...a departure from the surrealistic verse more common to my high school writings."

Alexis Kielb
Community High School, Ann Arbor, Michigan, 2000
Alexis Kielb is a student at the University of Minnesota majoring in English literature and creative writing. After having spent a term in England, she strongly suspects that Wales is the most beautiful and least visited country in Britain. Ultimately she wants to get an MFA in writing.

Beth Kinderman
North High School, Eau Claire, Wisconsin, 2000
Beth Kinderman is a junior at St. Olaf College in Northfield, Minnesota, majoring in English and Spanish. She is still writing poetry and has published work in a number of journals. She also writes essays, creative non-fiction, and, under the moniker "gamerchick," a bi-weekly column for gamegrene.com, an online magazine about role-playing games. In her spare time she contributes to roleplayingtips.com, maintains a personal web site, and works as a lighting technician in St. Olaf's Theatre Department.

Vanessa Kogan
Nyack High School, Upper Nyack, New York, 1999
Vanessa Kogan is currently a third-year student at Barnard College, Columbia University, majoring in comparative literature. Since graduating high school she has worked in France and Macedonia, and traveled through the Balkans and eastern Europe. She is an editor and contributing writer on the staff of the *Columbia Review.* As we went to press, she was hoping to study full time at the Smolny Institute in Saint Petersburg, Russia.

David J. Konieczkowski
University School, Hunting Valley, Ohio, 2002
David Konieczkowski is currently a freshman and prospective molecular biology major at Princeton University. The three pieces in this anthology were written during the summer of 2000 under the wing of Peter Markus and the Creative Writing Institute at Interlochen Arts Camp, Michigan. In 2001, under David Rybicki, he received Interlochen's Fine Arts Award for Poetry. His work has also been published in the *Louisville Review*. In his free time at Princeton, David plays trumpet for several university ensembles, writes for a student-run foreign policy magazine, and works as a chemistry study group leader.

Zoe Konovalov
Anglo-American School, U.S. Embassy, Moscow, 1997
After graduation from Yale in 2001, Zoe Konovalov now works as an analyst for the investment firm Dean & Company in Washington, D.C.

Andrew (Drew) Krewer
Interlochen Arts Academy, Interlochen, Michigan, 2001
Andrew Krewer was raised in rural Georgia and attended New York University and Interlochen Arts Academy. Currently a student at Oberlin College, he intends to major in creative writing. He has work forthcoming in *Quick Fiction* and *Seems*.

Nora Lawrence
Hunter College High School, New York City, 1997
Nora Lawrence attended Pomona College in Claremont, California, where she was editor-in-chief of the *Student Life* newspaper and coordinator of the student art society. She is now living in Los Angeles and pursuing a PhD in art history at the University of Southern California.

Natasha Le Bel
Saint Ann's School, Brooklyn, New York, 1994
As an undergraduate at Yale, Natasha Le Bel received the James Ashmun Veech Prize, the Gordon Barber Memorial Prize in Poetry, and the Peter J. Wallace Memorial Prize for non-fiction. As a senior, she represented Yale as one of five Connecticut Circuit Student Poets participating in a reading tour of Connecticut colleges and universities. After her 1998 graduation with a BA in art history, she spent three years in Washington, DC, working at a local art gallery and at the Corcoran Gallery of Art. Currently living in Manhattan with her husband Stefan, and working as a publicist in the Arts and Communications Counselors division of Ruder Finn, Inc, she is also on the advisory board of the *Saint Ann's Review,* a journal of arts and literature founded by her high school writing teacher Beth Bosworth.

Annie Lee
Parsippany Hills High School, Parsippany New Jersey, 1999
Annie Lee is currently a senior at Princeton University, studying texts in English, Chinese, and French, and majoring in comparative literature. She has published in the *Asian Pacific American Journal* and *Cymbals,* a national student literary magazine. University awards

include the President's Award for Academic Excellence, freshman and sophomore awards in creative writing, and the Ward Mathis Short Story Award. She also received a Martin Dale Fellowship to spend a summer in Beijing learning calligraphy and writing poetic responses to Chinese characters. While there she also taught conversational English through the Princeton-in-Asia program. In her spare time, she enjoys cooking and belly dancing. She is editor of the *Nassau Literary Review.*

Ben Lerner
Topeka High School, Topeka, Kansas, 1997
Ben Lerner graduated with a BA in political science from Brown University in 2001, where he is now completing his MFA in poetry. While at Brown he has won five creative writing prizes; his poems can be found in recent or forthcoming editions of the *Beloit Poetry Journal.* the *Denver Quarterly*, the *Paris Review*, *Ploughshares*, the *Threepenny Review*, *Verse*, and *Slate*. He co-founded and co-edits *No: A Journal of the Arts*, a magazine of poetry, criticism, and images scheduled to debut in early 2003.

Christopher Lew
Stuyvesant High School, New York City, 1999
Christopher Lew has attended Rice University in Houston,, Texas, and Saint Louis University in Madrid, Spain. He is currently finishing his undergraduate work in English and Spanish literature at New York University's Gallatin School of Individualized Study.

Mike Livshits
Stuyvesant High School, New York City, 2001
Mike Livshits studied writing with Douglas Goetsch while at Stuyvesant. He is currently a student at McGill University in Montreal.

H. Katharine Lo
Castilleja School, Palo Alto, California, 2000
H. Katharine Lo is currently a junior psychology major at Dartmouth College. A Presidential Scholar, she does research with a psychology professor on intergroup contact experience. She has continued with her musical interests, playing principal flute in the Dartmouth Symphony Orchestra; and she is a member of Delta Delta Delta sorority.

Billy Lopez
Hunter College High School, New York City, 1999
Billy Lopez is in his senior year at Amherst College, majoring in English. He has been awarded three prizes by the faculty for his poetry. He plays guitar, bass and drums in various rock bands.

Grace Lorentz
Madison East High School, Madison, Wisconsin, 1997
Grace Lorentz is presently studying at the American University in Cairo. She attended the University of California at Berkeley for one year, then an art school in San Francisco another year, where she stud-

ied illustration. She then took time off, lived in London and eventually returned home where she enrolled at the University of Wisconsin Madison. She expects to graduate in 2003 with a degree in religious studies.

Erica Magrey
Southington High School, Southington, Connecticut, 1995
Erica Magrey attended art school at the University of Hartford, graduating *summa cum laude* with a BFA in photography. She represented the University on the Connecticut Poetry Circuit in 1997, as well as receiving the Felicia A. Miller Award for excellence in art, and the Helen Cheney Martyn Prize for excellence in photography. Since graduation she has assisted a professional photographer, managed part of a custom lab, done freelance photography and writing, and taught both art and photography, while also showing her work at several group shows and a solo exhibition. She currently works as an editor at *The Princeton Review*, a New York City-based educational company.

Bob Meyer
Justin Siena High School, 1994
After high school Bob Meyer majored in English at UC Berkeley. He is currently attending law school at the University of Oregon. A road trip to Seattle with some friends inspired him to start writing again, compelled to record what had happened though it quickly turned into fiction. He is currently taking a fiction-writing class at the University, which he finds to be a great release from the tensions of law school.

Michael Mirer
Cass Technical High School, Detroit, Michigan, 1998

Bruce A. Morris, Jr.
Wheeling High School, Wheeling, Illinois, 1995
After graduation from Illinois State University, Bruce A. Morris, Jr. went to work as a police officer for the village of Palatine. Currently he is pursuing a master's degree in urban development at DePaul University.

Matthew Moses
Edward R. Murrow High School, Brooklyn, New York, 1997
Matthew Moses graduated *magna cum laude* from Binghamton University in 2001, with a major in creative writing and a minor in theater. He's had poems published in *American Poet*, the *Brooklyn Review* and *Harpur Palate*. While in college he wrote and directed the one-act plays *Couples Eating, The Humbling,* and *Between the Spaces Between Our Homes,* and wrote an adaptation of Sophocles' *Electra*. He is currently the assistant to the executive producer at *The Daily Show*. He studies and performs improv comedy at the Upright Citizens Brigade Theater in New York. He recently completed his first full-length play, *Daniella Uses Dirty Words*.

Talia Neffson
Packer Collegiate Institute, Brooklyn, New York, 1999

Sara A. Newland
Hunter College High School, New York City, 2000
Sara Newland is a senior political science major at Wellesley College, where she has studied poetry with Frank Bidart and creative non-fiction with Pankaj Mishra. Her honors thesis is on the development of the juvenile justice system in the United States.

Katie Nichol
Perpich Center for Arts Education, Golden Valley, Minnesota, 2000
Katie Nichol has recently found a home in St. Paul, Minnesota ,where she is writing poems and working with street-dependent youth. Since graduating high school she has spent equal amounts of time at Beloit College, where she was awarded the White Howells Honorable Mention for Poetry, and in Columbia, South Carolina, with AmeriCorps. She plans on returning to college within the next year to major in creative writing and community studies.

Rina Nilooban
John P. Stevens High School, Edison, New Jersey, 1996
Rina Nilooban participated in the Middlesex County Arts High School and the New Jersey School of the Arts at Montclair State University.

Sarah Nooter
Saint Ann's School, Brooklyn, New York, 1996
Sarah Nooter attended Amherst College where she majored in classics and English. She won the Academy of American Poets Prize and the Laura Ayres Snyder Poetry Prize, the William C. Collar Prize in Greek, and the MacArthur-Leithauser Travel Award. She graduated in 2001and received the American Philological Society's Lionel Pearson Fellowship to do postgraduate study in classics at an English or Scottish university.

Emily Parker
Saint Ann's School, Brooklyn, New York, 1995
Emily Parker graduated with honors from Brown University with a double major in international relations (diplomacy) and comparative literature (with a focus on French and Spanish literature). She spent almost three years living in China and Japan. She is currently a master's candidate in East Asian Studies at Harvard University's Graduate School of Arts and Sciences.

Benjamin C. Patton
Lakeside High School, Seattle, Washington, 1999
Benjamin C. Patton is studying at Stanford University, where he is a double major in East Asian Studies and Symbolic Systems. He spent the summer of 2001 studying Japanese at Middlebury College, then went directly to Kyoto, Japan, for a junior year abroad. After finishing the first semester he left school for a year to apprentice with Takashi

Nakazato, a well-known ceramics artist in Karatsu. He was due to finish his year of manual labor in December, 2002, then return to Stanford to continue as before with academics and riding for Stanford's cycling team; though now, he says, "I might throw in some political activism, for peace, on the side...."

Phoebe Prioleau
Trinity School, New York City, 2002
Phoebe Prioleau attends Stanford University, where she writes for the *Stanford Daily*. Poetry has been her passion for as long as she can remember. Her work has appeared in *Thumbprints*, the *Claremont Review*, *Tucumcarie Literary Review* and *Creative Juices*. During a year abroad at an English boarding school, she edited the youth supplement to the town newspaper, *The Petersfield Post*.

Joey Roth
Montclair High School, Montclair, New Jersey, 2001
Joey Roth was co-editor-in-chief of Montclair High School's literary journal. He concentrated on writing short fiction. He tells us that he actually prefers reading poems to writing them.

Quentin Rowan
Friends Seminary, Brooklyn, New York, 1994
Quentin Rowan attended Oberlin College where he majored in English and played in a variety of rock bands. His fiction has since appeared in the *Paris Review*, among other places.

Renada Rutmanis
Southwest High School, Minneapolis, Minnesota, 1998
Renada Rutmanis graduated from UC Berkeley with a bachelor's degree in English in 2001. She then moved to New York City, where she interned at several magazines, including *Premier* and *Entertainment Weekly*. She attended the Breadloaf Writers Conference in 2002, and plans to enroll in an MFA program for fiction in 2004.

Julia Schaffer
Saint Ann's School, Brooklyn, New York, 1995
Since graduation from Brown University in 1999, Julia Schaffer has worked as a writer of speeches and greeting cards as well as poems and plays. Her solo show, *Hold the Floor*, played at the Henry Street Settlement and Atlantic Theatre Company studios as well as in Germany. Her children's play, *In the Bedroom of Toots and Company*, received its first performance under the aegis of New York City's Parks Department after-school program, where she teaches drama. She is a big fan of several Saint Ann's writing teachers and remains in their debt.

Julie Anne Scharper
Notre Dame Preparatory School, Lutherville, Maryland, 1997
Julie Anne Scharper went on after high school to study at Johns Hopkins University.

Rebecca Schonberg
Hunter College High School, New York City, 2001
Rebecca Schonberg is currently majoring in comparative literature at Cornell University. She has continued to write on her own and has taken creative writing classes at Cornell. She has had poems published in the *Susquehanna Review* and in *Rainy Day*, an on-campus literary magazine.

Rachel Schwartz
Wheeling High School, Wheeling, Illinois, 1995

Anna Soo-Hoo
Brooklyn Technical High School, Brooklyn, New York, 1995
Anna Soo-Hoo has published work in *Poetry in Performance*. She is presently trying to get herself to write an essay.

Deborah Stein
Hunter College High School, New York City, 1995
Deborah Stein won an award for her work from the City College High School Poetry Festival; she went on to study poetry at the University of Virginia's Young Writers Workshop.

Alison Stine
Lexington High School, Mansfield, Ohio, 1996
Alison Stine's poems appeared in the New Voices section of the *Kenyon Review* in Summer/Fall 1999. She has work forthcoming in the *Paris Review* and *Black Warrior Review*. Her chapbook, *Lot of My Sister*, winner of the Wick Prize, was published in 2001 by the Kent State University Press.

Emma Straub
Saint Ann's School, Brooklyn, New York, 1998
After graduating from Saint Ann's, Emma Straub attended Oberlin College. Her poetry has appeared in such publications as the *Boston Review*, *Boog City*, and *Small Spiral Notebook*, and on the website *The Spook*, of which she is also poetry editor. She is currently living in New York City and working on her first novel.

Shayna Strom
The Baldwin School, Bryn Mawr, Pennsylvania, 1998
In May 2002, Shayna Strom graduated *summa cum laude* and Phi Beta Kappa from Yale University, where she received her BA in Ethics, Politics, and Economics. At Yale she was the recipient of many scholastic and extracurricular awards, including the Roosevelt Thompson prize for the graduating senior with the strongest record of public service. While she envisions a career focusing on urban poverty issues, she is still an avid reader and writer of poetry; and is now pursuing doctoral study at Oxford University, as the recipient of a 2002 Rhodes Scholarship.

Mark Tanno
Stuyvesant High School, New York City, 1996
Mark Tanno graduated as an English major from Williams College in 2000, and is currently working for a public relations firm in New York City. Long-term plans include getting an MFA in creative writing over the next few years.

Drew Tarlow
Trinity High School, New York City, 2001
Drew Tarlow is currently a sophomore at Amherst College, majoring in political science. He continues to write, both fiction and poetry, and he says that, for helping him become passionate about writing, he owes many thanks to Bill Zavatsky, poet and teacher at his high school. He is also the managing editor for Amherst's political science magazine, the *Indicator*, and a section editor for the school's newspaper, the *Amherst Student*, and a member of the varsity tennis team.

Amara Dante Verona
Home Schooled, Madison, Wisconsin, 2001
Amara Dante Verona is currently co-editor of the literary journal, *The Styles*. She attends the University of Wisconsin at Madison as a film studies major and is working on her first screenplay, *The Successful Weatherman*. Various short films of hers have been shown in the Madison community. She is also working on a documentary about what it is like to start up a literary journal and all of the "wacky things that go on during the seemingly banal process of sorting through submissions, laying out the publication, and working with printers and bookstores." The look of printed matter is an obsession of hers. She lives in Madison with her sister and two chinchillas.

Erin Walsh
Raytown High School, Kansas City, Missouri, 1996

Lindsay Washick
MMI Preparatory School, Freeland, Pennsylvania, 2000
Lindsay Washick attends the Gallatin School of Individualized Study at New York University, studying documentary filmmaking and the impact of media on culture. She is an intern at MTV's News and Documentary Division, currently doing postproduction on a two-hour special that is scheduled to air early in 2003. After graduation next spring, she wants to continue to do production and editing for documentaries of all kinds and to keep living in New York.

Eric Wubbels
Bruton High School, Williamsburg, Virginia, 1997
Eric Wubbels majored in music at Amherst College, where he also pursued studies in linguistics and Japanese. At Amherst, he co-founded the New Music Ensemble and composed music using computers for both composition and presentation of his work. He graduated in 2001 but remained at Amherst for a year as a teaching assistant. He is now pursuing graduate studies in music composition at the University of California San Diego.

Kurt Wubbels
Bruton High School, Williamsburg, Virginia, 1996
Kurt Wubbels graduated from Bard College in May, 2000, with a degree in French literature, and is now living in Rhode Island.

Sharon Zetter
East Brunswick High School, East Brunswick, New Jersey, 2000
While in high school Sharon Zetter studied creative writing with Denise Duhamel at the New Jersey Governor's School of the Arts.